The Political Punter
How to make money
betting on politics

Mike Smithson

Hh

HARRIMAN HOUSE LTD

3A Penns Road
Petersfield
Hampshire
GU32 2EW

Tel: +44 (0)1730 233870
Fax: +44 (0)1730 233880

First published in Great Britain in 2007,
Copyright © Harriman House Ltd.

The right of Mike Smithson to be identified as Author has been asserted in accordance with
the Copyright, Design and Patents Act 1988
ISBN: 1905641095
ISBN 13: 978-1-905641-09-3
British Library Cataloguing in Publication Data
A CIP catalogue record for this book can be obtained from the British Library.

Printed and bound in Great Britain by Biddles Ltd, Kings Lynn, Norfolk

Contents

Preface   i

Introduction   1

1. Political Betting – An Overview   5

2. Choosing the Right Betting Vehicle   25

3. Betting Tactics – UK General Elections   61

4. Betting Tactics – Other Major Markets   79

5. Betting Tactics – Following the Betting   101

6. Betting Tactics – Following the Polls   121

7. The Process of Betting – The Key Decisions
   That Have to be Taken   145

8. Ten Tips for Profitable Political Betting   161

Appendices   167

Preface

What the book covers

This book is about gambling on politics. It explains the basics of how and where to gamble and then goes on to look at the characteristics of the main markets.

It looks at ways that opinion polls can be used effectively, as well as advice on identifying betting trends that might lead to profitable outcomes.

The main betting activity that is described is in the UK, the country with some of the most sophisticated and innovative betting operations in the world which attract customers from many different countries. Compared with many other countries UK gambling operates within a relatively light regulatory environment and has one of the most favourable tax regimes for punters.

Although UK politics is the primary focus, the book covers other countries where there is a big betting interest, notably the US and Europe.

Who the book is for?

This book has been designed for three groups of people:-

- Those who regularly bet on politics.

- Those with a keen interest in politics and who are attracted to the idea of using their knowledge for potential profit.

- Those who gamble in non-political markets who would like to extend their operations into the political arena.

For those who already bet on political matters the book includes a number of case histories where it is hoped that the lessons of the past might be helpful for the future. It is also hoped that the explanations of the mechanics of different forms of betting and a wide range of betting options will make people feel more confident to try new things.

For those non-gamblers with a keen interest in politics it is hoped that the book will provide enough background to allow them to dabble a bit and to get a better feel about possible political outcomes by understanding how those who are backing their opinions with cash are actually thinking.

For people who gamble and would like to know more about political betting it is hoped that the book will provide an information platform so that they can be more confident about risking their money in a new arena.

How the book is structured

The opening chapter has been designed to give an overview of political betting by looking at what gambling is, how it has developed and what are the possibilities now.

What the examples in the first chapter do not do is explain the mechanics of the betting which some can find confusing. That is covered in the following chapters when we will return to each of them again.

Chapters 2–6 go through the critical decisions that have to be taken when you want to bet.

Finally, the book has a list of the basic information sources that are there to help you come to a decision.

Finally, some thanks

This book would not have happened without the foresight and advice of Stephen Eckett of Harriman House. I have also been helped by Anthony Wells who runs UK Polling Report and Peter Smith who contributes articles on gambling to the Politicalbetting.com website. Thanks to Bestbetting.com for use of the site's historical odds and charting facilities.

Thanks also to my brother and sister-in-law, John and Judy, for allowing me to use their sea-front apartment in Aldeburgh in Suffolk as a peaceful place to write and to my son, Robert, who first suggested the idea in 2004 of me establishing a blog on political betting.

Introduction

At just after 11pm on the night before the May 2005 general election a retired solicitor and staunch Methodist, who is strongly opposed to gambling, knocked on my door with £500 in twenty pound notes in his hand. Could I, he asked, put a bet on for him? He explained that for the past three weeks he had been doing a daily 200 mile round trip to help the Liberal Democrats in the North Norfolk constituency, where the prominent blogger and then owner of the Politico's bookstore, Iain Dale, had been running a high profile campaign to try to recapture the seat lost by Conservatives four years earlier.

"But Patrick", I replied, "gambling is against your religion and you have never put a bet on in your life". "Yes I have been thinking about that," was his response, "but it is only a gamble if there is an element of risk involved. We are going to hold on to the seat by a shed load of votes tomorrow and it would be wrong for me not to make a little profit on it".

However, the hard fact that usually only the bookmakers win in the end and the gamblers usually lose applies to the body of all *punters* – the term used in this book to describe those who wish to bet on political outcomes. But what is clear is that over time the performance of some punters is greater than others and those with good political skills and an understanding of how betting markets operate can and do make money.

The objective of this book is to assist readers in becoming part of that winning group and to enjoy themselves at the same time.

The latter is an important element. For many, the great satisfaction of betting on political outcomes is not just the money but the pleasure of being proved right. Anybody can have an opinion about a political outcome. The gambler has put money behind it and winning is a way of validating your judgment.

In 2005 I got enormous pleasure out, as well as a lot of cash, of spotting the potential of David Cameron for the Tory leadership and getting a bet on at 5/1 some four months before he won and while most people were regarding David Davis's bid as a foregone conclusion. Even to be partially right is pleasant. As I write this in February 2007 the black senator from Illinois, Barack Obama, has suddenly burst onto the US political scene and is second favourite to win the Democratic nomination for the 2008 White House race. Getting on for two years earlier, in May 2005, I had been looking over possible presidential candidates and had decided to put £50 on him at the then price of 50/1. Even if he does not make it all the way in 2008, I will still feel good from having spotted that he did have the potential to be a serious challenger.

Political Betting

An Overview

1
Political Betting
An Overview

From the days of gentlemen's wagers

On a window sill in the corner of the Smoking Room in Magdalen College, Oxford, there is a wonderful ancient leather-bound volume that at first sight looks like an old Bible but is in fact a testament to the long-standing and deep-seated desire of people to bet money or items of value on events with an uncertain outcome.

For on close inspection you will find the words "Betting Book" embossed in gold leaf on the cover and inside there is a record of wagers going back generations on a huge range of events and points of fact. Clearly there has been a book like this there for centuries and what is recorded inside gives a fascinating insight about what people were arguing about at different times in history and on what they were prepared to bet.

As an example, entries in the Magdalen book dated the 17th and 18th of August 1940 record bets that two members of the college made with each other at the height of the Battle of Britain. Written out in long-hand is the following,

Bet made 17 August: Dr Griffiths bets Dr Rollin one pint of beer that 150 or more German aeroplanes will be brought down over the country on Saturday August 17th 1940. Paid by Dr Griffiths 17.8.1940

Above bet renewed for Sunday August 18th 1940. Paid by Dr Rollin.

Although not obviously a political bet this wager related to something that had enormous political significance. One of the parties in this case, Dr James Griffiths, was a physicist who had worked on radar. Whether or not the bet was made on the basis of any special knowledge one can only speculate.

Even today, with sophisticated online betting structures available round the clock, the tradition of the wager still thrives. For whenever friends, colleagues or families get together there can be fierce arguments about a future happening. One party puts forward a proposition that is strongly challenged and this often leads to one of them saying "I'll bet you". Agreeing to a wager is a good way of resolving the issue. Both parties are able to demonstrate through the process how much they believe in their view. It also gets to the heart of what a lot of political betting is about – it is a way of proving that your judgment about how a future event is better than somebody else's. This activity is not just about money.

Political betting until 1961 – on the margins of legality

As a betting vehicle, of course, the wager has two big limitations. Firstly, they are almost always for even money – that is, the amount the winning party receives is the same for each side irrespective of the chances of the event happening. Secondly, you can only make your bet if you can find somebody else prepared to accept it.

Betting always requires two parties: the person making the bet and the person or organisation who is, in betting parlance, prepared to "lay" it. If you win, the layer of the bet pays you while, if you lose, the layer keeps your stake.

It is here that bookmakers fill the gap. They are there to offer "odds" – that is to set out what they will pay you if you are right in your prediction, and to lay bets on a wide range of different options. Without them the possibilities for betting would be very limited indeed. They aim to make their money by accepting bets on all the possibilities (or "runners") in an event and adjusting the odds they offer so that whatever the outcome they end up in profit.

In most countries there have been, and still are, very strict legal controls on betting, and even in the UK legalised bookmakers with offices in every high street are a relatively modern phenomenon. Until 1961 there were few legal ways in which it was possible to have a bet with a bookmaker. You could go to a racecourse and risk your money with one of the on course bookmakers, or you could bet there on the Tote. The other option was to have an account with a telephone bookmaker. The latter were not very widespread because, in those days, there was no means of using a credit or charge card (which did not then exist) to make a payment. The process of applying for an account was quite cumbersome and you either made a deposit or the bookmaker had to trust your creditworthiness.

Central to the concept of a bet is that it is not a legally enforceable contract. So you cannot sue the bookmaker, and the bookmaker cannot sue you if you fail to pay. This is why punters, both then and now, are invariably asked to put money up front; every time they hand over their stake money they are taking a gamble on a bookmaker's honesty and solvency.

This was particularly important in the pre-legalisation days. For, away from the world of telephone bookmakers and racetracks, there developed a grey area of bookmakers operating illegally throughout the UK, who would be supported by an elaborate network of what were known as "bookies' runners". The latter would be there in pubs, workplaces and other locations at a certain time and would provide the link between the punter and the person ready to lay the bets.

This practise was prevalent in almost every locality and although the focus was on sporting events, particularly horse racing, there were lots of opportunities to bet on the big political events of the day, particularly general elections and party leadership battles.

Inevitably this tended to attract criminal elements, which affected the whole way that society perceived what was taking place.

All change in 1961 – the legalisation of betting

Legislation came into effect in 1961 that for the first time legalised large parts of the betting industry, including the high street betting shop. For the first time you could pop into one of the new shops, place your bet and listen as a commentary on each race was broadcast on loudspeakers (known as the "blower"). The new premises were fairly Spartan places. In order to discourage people from spending long periods of time there, the law restricted the shops to few facilities and they therefore tended to become rather unattractive environments.

The critical thing, though, was that you could bet, and the newly legal bookmaking profession began to develop all sorts of means to attract punters and, the lack of comfort notwithstanding, to get people into their shops.

The first legal political markets

Within fifteen months came the first big legal political betting event, following the sudden death of the Labour leader, Hugh Gaitskell, on January 18th 1963 at the age of 56. Three candidates fought for the office: James Callaghan, George Brown and Harold Wilson – for the first time, punters were able to pop into betting shops and back their fancy just like in a horse race. This was before the days of mass membership ballots in the party and the decision was totally in the hands of MPs. Wilson, who had challenged Gaitskell just three years earlier, was seen as having a strong chance from the start and became a betting favourite. He won with a comfortable margin.

The resignation of Harold Macmillan

However, the amount of gambling on that was nothing like on the scale of what was to happen eight months later following the resignation, on health grounds, of the Prime Minister, Harold Macmillan. The political atmosphere had already been stoked up by the Profumo affair that had dominated the headlines for months. News of Macmillan's resignation came at the time of the 1963 Conservative Party Conference, which rapidly became something akin to an American political convention as various candidates and their supporters jostled publicly to stake their claims.

A challenge for punters was that the Conservative Party had no formal procedure for selecting a leader, merely a series of confused precedents about how a candidate would "emerge" and the Queen was expected to choose on the basis of advice given by the Party's elder statesmen. There were no opinion polls of this group and it was very hard for all but the chosen few to judge how the process would work out.

This did not stop speculation or the gambling, and for the bookmakers the contest proved to be extraordinarily profitable. As secret discussions were taking place the money piled on Rab Butler, who was the preferred choice of Tory MPs and had been seen as the heir apparent for years. Another high profile candidate, Quintin Hogg, then Lord Hailsham, launched his bid in an emotionally charged speech that was nationally televised and he seemed to have many amongst the party membership behind him. Both had very short prices and the media was presenting this as a battle between the two. It was not to be. The eventual winner,

Alex Douglas-Home, who was then an Earl, appeared to come from nowhere and this was reflected in his betting price.

At the time I was a still at school and recall being so impressed by the Hailsham TV speech that, even though I was below the legal age for betting, I decided to put on some of my pocket money. The following lunchtime, wearing my school blazer, I popped into a bookmaker's shop for the very first time to place a bet of what was known in those pre-decimal days as "half a crown" (12.5 pence) at a price that I think was either 3/1 or 7/2. I certainly remember calculating that I would get, with my stake, at least "ten bob" (50 pence) back. Sadly, this was not to be, and the bet, like many others that were to follow, was a loser.

October 1964 – the first legal general election betting

October 1964 had all the makings of a good general election for the bookmakers, for punters generally find elections that are close very appealing, especially if there is a real prospect of a change of government. And this was the first general election where you could pop into one of the high street shops and have a flutter.

After the media batterings that the Government had suffered, there was a view that the Tory years were coming to an end. Wilson had presented himself as a "man of the people" – something that had been helped by the vast increase in television ownership in the previous five years and the development of the first modern style news and current affairs programmes.

Would Labour under its new leader, Harold Wilson, manage to seize back power from Sir Alec Douglas-Home's Conservative party, and what would be the scale of the majority? The victory was seen by many as almost a foregone conclusion and Labour was ahead in the polls. A lot of the betting was on the size of the Labour majority and the number of seats that the main parties would win. Special general election betting forms were available in many bookmakers and you could bet on the size of the majority in 15 seat blocks. Thus there was a price on Labour by 1-15 seats, 16-30 and so on.

The end result, Labour by a miniscule majority, came as a shock because all the signs were that Wilson's party was going to do so much better than it did. But it was a profitable Thursday for Britain's growing bookmaker community. And, within two years, Wilson had to go to the country again, when he secured a working majority.

The 1970 general election – when the favourite fell at the last fence

All assumed in 1970 that Harold Wilson would steam to an easy victory in the general election which took place bang in the middle of the football World Cup – when England was defending the trophy won four years earlier. Labour was a strong odds-on favourite to come out on top and enjoyed reasonable poll standings.

Wilson could have waited until the following year but feared that the party might have been hit by the introduction of decimalisation of the currency, which was scheduled for February 15th 1971, and a delay would have left him without room for late changes. Despite warnings against holding an election in the middle of the World Cup, he opted for June 18th.

As it turned out the week of the general election coincided with England's quarter-final World Cup match in Mexico against the defeated finalist of 1966, West Germany. Emotions were running high and the bookmakers did a good trade accepting what are known as "doubles" – where punters sought to increase their return from England beating West Germany by linking it with a bet on Labour wining the general election.

Neither side of this gamble worked. West Germany scored a third goal in extra time – England were out of the World Cup – and three days later Labour lost the general election. Again, the bookmakers were very happy and that week proved to be a bonanza for them. A common explanation for Labour's unexpected defeat was the knock-on effect of England's defeat. Who knows? But since then no general election has coincided with a major sporting event.

November 2004 – when political betting came of age

Almost every political gambler has a story to tell of what happened overnight on that first Tuesday in November 2004, when George W. Bush was seeking to win a second term at the White House in the face of a strong challenge from the Democrat, John Kerry.

The amounts of money that changed hands were colossal – much of it moving in the space of a very short time. On the Betfair betting exchange alone, which has made figures public, over £17m was traded on the "which party would win the Presidential Election" bet – the vast bulk in just a few hours after leaks about exit polls, and then the polls themselves seeming to suggest that Kerry had done it.

The traditional bookmakers and the spread betting firms all reported record activity in the non-sports market and my estimate is that in the UK alone in excess of £30m-£40m was gambled.

From the start this had all the makings of a big market. The question of who occupies the White House has an effect on the entire world and there is no more important election. This was accentuated by the events of the previous three years, particularly the divisions in many countries over the war in Iraq.

Added to that was the personal factor. People like to bet on personalities that they think they know and there is nothing that fires political gamblers up more than an apparent close race.

As the evening wore on unoffiicial reports began emerging on the internet about the exit polls (surveys asking people how they voted as they leave the polling stations). These were not due to be announced officially until the polls had closed in the East Coast states, but information seeped out.

What was happening, it was suggested, was in direct contradiction of the final polls of the campaign which had been predicting a Bush victory. So suddenly, in the space of a very short time, there was a massive push to get money on Kerry and the Democrats. The prices tightened to an extraordinary extent. People wanted to believe those exit surveys and they wanted to cash in.

The danger of personal bias

For me – perhaps like many others – I had let my personal feelings about George W. Bush distort my judgment. In the months leading up to November I had spent hours scrutinising the operations and history of every pollster that carried out White House race surveys for evidence that suggested that the Bush lead that was being forecast was wrong. When a pollster reported a Kerry lead, I scoured the internet for data that would support the view that that particular firm could be taken more seriously.

On the election day itself I had continued to back Kerry, as reports of big queues outside polling stations in key states pointed, correctly as it transpired, to a very high turnout. My assumption, wrong as it turned out, was that the Democrat would be the beneficiary.

The exit poll news had a dramatic effect on the betting, so that by 11.15pm UK time the most winnings you could expect for a £100 Kerry bet was £35. At the start of the day such a wager would have produced £120.

Thankfully at that point I began to get cold feet. My recall was that similar unofficial reports of the exit polls four years earlier had put Al

Gore well ahead – I opted to play safe. In a flash I got out and sold my entire position at what were still favourable terms.

By midnight my potential winnings on a Kerry victory were down to 60% of what they had been a quarter of an hour earlier, but I had managed to arrange my betting so I stood to lose absolutely nothing at all if Bush won.

I was fortunate, but a lot of people lost a lot of money that night.

Political betting becomes mainstream

For the bookmakers the White House race meant political betting had grown up. It was a serious area which was worth them putting time and effort into, and for the following UK general election they created more betting options than ever before.

All this encouraged the media to take the activity seriously. During the run-up to the 2005 UK general election, one newspaper, the Daily Telegraph, began including on its city pages every day the latest betting prices on the overall outcome and the Commons seat spreads from the spread betting firms. I was commissioned by the paper to write regular reports on election betting.

As a gambling event, as the following table shows, the UK general election attracted about half as much money as the White House race, but it was still significant. These are the figures from just one operator, the betting exchange, Betfair, of the amounts traded on recent political events. The overall amounts bet across all the range of UK bookmakers would be several times larger.

Date traded	Event	Amount
November 2004	US Presidential election	£17,849,232
May 2005	General election	£8,473,661
December 2005	Tory leadership race	£2,054,419
March 2006	Liberal Democrats leadership race	£1,000,382
April 2006	Italian Presidential election	£1,790,547
November 2006	US Midterms	£497,708

The table is interesting in that it shows what turns political punters on.

What excites political punters?

The biggest elections in 2006 by far, in terms of global importance, were the US Midterms, when the ability of President George W. Bush to govern was severely limited by his party, the Republicans, losing control of Congress and the Senate. This was covered widely by the media across the world and, in particular, the UK where, of course, there was the advantage that all the main players spoke English.

The amount of information about the vote, the issues and the candidates coming out of the US in the months leading up to November 6th was enormous. All the main UK news channels devoted hours of coverage.

Yet these elections attracted only relatively moderate interest amongst British political gamblers, who two years earlier had made the Kerry-Bush White House race the biggest political gambling event ever.

This was despite the fact that the result was a complete turnaround from what had looked likely only a couple of months beforehand; and the eventual outcome of which party would control the Senate was tight right until the end.

This relative lack of interest was not because it was about something going on in a foreign country. The biggest UK betting event of that year was the Italian general election, which received fairly scant coverage in the domestic media. In fact, on the Italian election night, April 9/10, there was only a fraction of the coverage on the UK news channels compared with what was seen from the US seven months later.

Ranking some way behind Italy in terms of UK betting interest was the leadership race for who should replace Charles Kennedy at the head of the third party, the Liberal Democrats.

What made the Italian election and its aftermath so compelling to punters was that it was a battle of titans between two politicians well known in the UK and throughout Europe: Silvano Berlusconi, the media magnate turned politician, and Roman Prodi, former President of the European Union.

Initial exit polls suggested a victory for Prodi, but the results narrowed as the count progressed. Two days after the vote Prodi declared, but Berlusconi never conceded defeat explicitly (although this was not required by the Italian law).

It took a week and a half of fierce battles before Italy's court of last resort ruled that Prodi had indeed won the election, winning control of the Chamber of Deputies by only 24,755 votes out of more than 38 million votes cast.

The experience of all of this is that what makes a political event attractive to gamblers is when it involves personalities that they know and there is a very tight race.

Betting on opinion polls – a weekly market?

A real problem for political gamblers is that, away from general elections and party leadership contests, there is a relative lack of things to bet on. Most of the time, the markets that are available will not come to a conclusion for months, or even years. People like to put money on this instant, and expect everything to be resolved in a matter of days, not the years that sometimes characterise political betting.

In early 2007 a weekly political betting market was launched in an attempt to meet the need for regular betting. Punters were asked to predict polling index numbers showing how leading politicians were perceived – would their popularity be going up or down?

The challenge was to create something that punters could bet on, confident that other punters, or the bookmaker, did not have inside knowledge.

Trading bets

For many people the idea of betting means placing a bet and then waiting for the result. For example, with a horse race a punter will place a bet before the race begins, and then wait to see which horse wins.

However, betting is no longer restricted to this.

The development of modern betting systems, such as the betting exchanges and spread-betting, together with the ability to operate 24/7 on the internet, has created opportunities for punters to *trade* bets, instead of having to wait for the final result. This allows punters to bet on changing sentiments about political outcomes.

When you trade a bet, you are not looking to the final outcome of an event, but whether you can make short-term to medium-term gains by predicting how you think *other* punters will react to the changing situation.

And this is just as well. For without it, political betting would be dull – placing a bet in, say, January and then potentially having to wait until May for the result!

In practice, betting prices are rising and falling all the time, reacting to the sentiment in the market. The new gambling systems allow you to get in and out of positions any time – thus creating the possibility of a short term profit if you have called it correctly.

You are aiming to back at a long price, in the hope of being able to lay a similar bet, when prices have tightened some time later. Or, conversely, lay a market first, and then back it when prices have widened.

Example

A punter may back Labour to win the next general election at a price of, say, 2/1. And this bet might be placed one year before the election itself.

Over the following two months, the news flow on Labour might be very positive, and the price on Labour tightens to evens (1/1).

At this point the punter may decide to take his profit by laying Labour to win at 1/1. His exposure to the market would then be neutral, because he would have equal and opposite bets in the market.

Having done this, the punter might then think that market sentiment has over-reacted and the price of 1/1 is just *too tight* for Labour to reflect Labour's real chances at the next election. And so the punter might think about additionally laying Labour at 1/1, thinking that their price is bound to widen at some point before the election. If the punter is correct, and the price does widen, then he would take his second profit by backing Labour (to neutralise his lay bet).

A difference in time-scales

In the above case, the punter laid Labour, even though he might think that *Labour was going to win the actual election*! This may seem contradictory – but it is not. It is simply a matter of different time frames.

- In the **long term** (to the election itself) the punter might think that Labour will win.

- But in the **short-term**, the punter thinks that the Labour betting price is temporarily too tight, and will weaken in the near term.

Irrational exuberance

Political, and sports betting are particularly good for sentiment trading, because amateur punters tend to bet with their heart and not their head. So, an amateur punter will tend to back the political party or the football team they support. When this happens *en masse* the betting price can tighten beyond a level that experienced punters think is realistic, and the latter will come into the market laying the bets on the other side. The experienced betters will always be happy to exploit the irrational exuberance of the crowd. A little while later, when the exuberance has died down and the prices have widened, the experienced betters will offset their earlier bets by backing the market and thereby taking their profit.

Real-life examples of trading bets can be seen at:

- Betfair: Case study – Betting exchange: cashing in your bet before the event has happened [p.42]

- Spread betting: Case study – Pocketing your profits even though your choice was a loser [p.52]

Choosing the Right
Betting Vehicle

2
Choosing the Right Betting Vehicle

Overview

This chapter looks at the range of betting vehicles that are now available and the possibilities they offer for political gamblers. What is remarkable is how extensive it is and how much of what is now there and accepted as part of the scene is so new.

Not so very long ago there simply was only one real option – the traditional bookmaker. Some people might have had telephone credit accounts, but they were a very few.

Two things changed everything – the internet, and the ability of people to transfer funds electronically in an instant from their credit cards or their bank accounts. The latter factor is critical. Since bookmakers cannot sue to recover gambling debts, they like cash up front. That is how high street bookmakers have always operated: no cash, no bet. Telephone and online card payments are what make modern betting systems possible.

The range of betting vehicles

The options for political betting are:

1. High street bookmakers

2. Accounts with traditional bookmakers

3. Betting exchanges

4. Deposit account spread betting

5. Credit account spread betting

These different betting types are explained below.

1. High street bookmakers

Advantages

*   Can be convenient.

*   No need to open accounts.

*   You bet in cash and get your winnings in cash.

*   Can often accept bets for larger amounts than available on the phone or online.

*   Sometimes local bookmakers will take bets on local matters not available elsewhere – it is possible to walk in and ask what odds will be available on a specialised proposition.

- Prices expressed in standard fractional format that most UK gamblers are familiar with.

Disadvantages

- Limited range of political markets.

- Often hard to find prices and compare.

- Mainly directed at sports betting and staff sometimes unfamiliar with political markets.

- Have to lock your stake up for a long time in long-term markets.

- You have to bet 'for' something rather than 'against'.

- Limited opening hours.

Suitability

Gamblers with all levels of experience.

2. Accounts with traditional bookmakers

Advantages

- Usually available online or by phone.

- Online betting usually available 24/7.

- Wider range of political markets than high street bookmakers.

- Easy to compare prices using the betting odds search engines.

- Attractive special offers usually available for new customers.

- Prices expressed in standard fractional format.

Disadvantages
- You usually have to open an account.

- Few options available to bet 'against' something rather than for.

- Your stake can be locked up for a long time in long-term markets like general elections.

- Once they have got your contact details they will bombard you with promotions.

- If you have a record of successful gambling with them it can often be hard to place bets. Understandably they prefer to accept bets from losing punters rather than known winning ones.

Suitability
Gamblers with all levels of experience apart from complete novices.

3. Betting exchanges

Advantages
- Available online 24/7.

- You can back and lay (bet against) any runner.

- Usually there is a good range of political markets.

- Generally better prices are available than with traditional bookmakers.

- You can get out of your position by betting in the opposite direction from your initial bet.

- If you have been right about the direction of the market you can sometimes get all your stake money out and still have open bets remaining.

- Betting usually continues right until a result is known – so bets can be taken on an election even while the count is taking place.

- There is sometimes scope for those with 'inside knowledge' to capitalise.

- The information available online from the betting exchanges is comprehensive with the price history and your own positions.

- Generally no restrictions are placed on successful punters.

Disadvantages

- The betting process can at first appear complex and difficult to understand.

- Because it is other punters who are accepting bets and not the bookmaker, your betting is limited by what other gamblers are prepared to accept.

- Prices expressed in the decimal format, which many gamblers find confusing.

- Occasionally the betting exchanges are not clear enough in defining the rules of a political market at the start and there can be big issues in the way an exchange settles the bets.

- Although you can gamble on the phone the nature of what you are doing makes betting online almost a necessity.

- You have to pay a commission on your net winnings.

- There has been a tendency for the exchanges to be less bold in establishing innovative and interesting markets.

Suitability

Suitable for gamblers with all levels of experience who are reasonably computer literate and numerate.

4. Deposit account spread betting

Advantages

- With spread betting the more you are right the more you win – and the more you are wrong the more you lose. Ideally suited to betting where the outcome can be expressed as a number – ie the total of seats parties will get in a general election.

- A spread, say on the number of seats, is quoted by the bookmaker and you can buy at the high figure and sell at the lower one.

- Prices move up and down and you can get out and take your profit even before the event has taken place. You can also close down a losing position at a smaller loss if you think it is going to go down further.

- Deposit accounts mean that your losses are limited to a "stop" level, though with most spread betting bookmakers there is no top limit.

- You can normally bet online.

- Accounts can usually be opened instantly.

Disadvantages
- Even with stop limits the potential for big losses can be quite large.

- You will be required to put up quite large sums to make a bet – money which is locked in until the event has happened or you decide to close your position.

- If you constantly win money the spread betting firms are likely to limit or even stop you betting altogether.

Suitability
This form of betting is not for the novice.

5. Credit account spread betting

Advantages
- All the main benefits of deposit account spread betting, except that you do not have to put money upfront.

- Ideally suited for long-term markets like general election outcomes where you can buy and sell as market sentiment changes and cash in your profits years before the outcome is known.

Disadvantages

- The downside risk is significant, and so a very disciplined approach to risk management is required.

- There is a complex application procedure before you will be accepted during which you have to show bank statements and other documents to prove your credit-worthiness.

Suitability

Ideal for the brave, the experienced and the rich.

Summary of different betting options

	Need for an account?	Close out positions early?	Prices expressed in...	Facility to Lay	Easy to compare prices?	Risk
High street bookmakers	No	No	Fractional odds (eg 6/4)	No	No	Low
Accounts with traditional bookmakers	Yes	No	Fractional odds (eg 6/4)	No	Yes	Low/med
Betting exchanges	Yes	Yes	Decimal (eg 2.5)	Yes	Yes	Med
Deposit account spread betting	Yes	Yes	Spreads (eg 65-68 seats)	Yes	No	Med
Credit account spread betting	Yes	Yes	Spreads (eg 65-68 seats)	Yes	No	Med/high

Traditional Betting

Traditional betting at your local betting shop

For decades the only real option if you wanted to place a political bet was to wander into your high street bookmaker with a pile of cash in your pocket. Many people still do this. The process is quite simple.

You take a betting slip from a dispenser, write out your selection on the form and hand it to one of the clerks with your stake money. The clerk checks it, takes your money and the two part slip is put into a machine where it is electronically stamped. One part is handed to you and the other is retained by the bookmaker. It is always important to check while you are still at the counter that the bet you think you are making is the bet that has been made. Rectifying things later – especially after the event – is nigh on impossible.

Your part of the slip has to be held onto until the outcome is known. If you have won, you pop into the shop again and exchange your slip for your winnings. All this is very simple and straightforward – provided you do not lose your betting slip in the meantime!

Political betting at the high street bookmaker

The main problem for political punters is that the shops are geared up for fast moving greyhound and horse-racing betting, and it is often difficult trying to do something out of the ordinary.

Sometimes your first challenge is to find out what the latest odds are for your chosen selection. In the final few days before an election there might be information on the electronic screens, and sometimes there are political odds quoted on the national bookmaker advertisements that are featured in the racing papers (pages of which are often pinned up on the walls).

Normally, though, there will be no data about political markets on display and you will have to queue and ask. In a busy shop when there are a lot of race meetings going on you do not make yourself popular if you tie up one of the clerks with something that they have to refer onwards, or check out the prices. It is probably wise to go in the morning.

Because you would have to go through this process with each bookmaker it can be particularly hard comparing the range of prices on offer.

The betting options are usually pretty limited. Thus if in a party leadership race you want to bet that Candidate A will not make it, then it is likely that you are going to have to bet for all the alternatives – Candidates B,C etc – to be certain of winning.

Another problem is that most political markets are long-term. Unlike a horse race, that is starting in ten minutes, it might be that a political bet is often on something that will not happen for years. You want to use your judgement about the way things will go but the idea of locking up your stake for a long time is not attractive.

Using the telephone or online services of a traditional bookmaker

All the major bookmaker firms have big telephone and online operations where you call, find out the odds, make your selection and normally use your credit or debit card to pay your stake. The range of markets is usually larger than you would find in a high street bookmaker.

To make a bet you need to open an account – the call centres are usually fairly slick in doing this quickly. You can either pay for each bet on each occasion or else make a deposit so you do not need to be giving your credit card details each time you phone. You can also do this online.

Normally any winnings are paid back into your account, where you have to initiate the process of withdrawing. With most firms you can either bet this way or use their internet facilities – the choice is yours.

If you want to compare prices, it is easier making a few calls to different telephone bookmakers than wandering along the high street. The call centres are equipped to give you information fast and if you do not proceed with a bet then that is not a problem.

To get any further with your phone call you will normally have to be registered with that bookmaker (the first question that you are asked is for your account details).

The telephone operations of the main bookmakers have all the limitations of the betting shops when it comes to the forms of betting that are possible.

An area where the telephone bookmakers with national call centres come into their own is in taking large bets which you might not be able to place in a shop or over the internet. Your request is usually channelled fairly quickly to one of the market specialists who will decide there and then the level at which they will allow you to go.

Thus, in the "Who is going to be the next Labour Deputy Leader" market in late 2006, the most I could get on my preferred choice with an internet bet was £33, whereas, on the phone a few minutes later, the same bookmaker was prepared to accept a bet of £200.

How bookmakers set the opening odds

The tricky part for a bookmaker is setting the opening prices; this is a highly skilled operation requiring a lot of knowledge of the area that is being covered. With sports betting there are a wide range of services to help them. With political betting it can be more challenging. The art for them is to create a market that has odds that are attractive enough to bring the punters in but from which the bookmaker will still make his profit.

Quite often with political betting, bargains can be had as soon as a new market is established. The bookmaker has had to make guesses as to what he thinks punters will be attracted to in order to get interest going – and his knowledge about the chances might not be as good as yours!

Betting Exchanges – Betting Against Other Punters

For many gamblers who have spent decades using traditional bookmakers the concept of a betting exchange is often quite hard to grasp.

It is self-evident that if you want to place a bet on a particular political outcome, then you need to find some organisation or individual who is prepared to lay it (take the risk of your prediction being correct) on terms that you find acceptable. Traditionally, as we have seen, the principle way of doing this was through the traditional bookmakers that take it upon themselves to assess the strengths of each runner in a market, issue a list of prices and accept bets.

Betting exchanges do not take any financial risk on the bets that go through them. They confine their role to providing a facility where those who want to bet for something are matched up with those who want to bet against (in betting exchange parlance to *lay*).

The betting exchange sets up and defines the markets, sits in the middle and when the outcome is known ensures payment to those who have got it right. Those who have been layers keep the stake money of backers who have placed losing bets and they pay out to the backers of those who have won.

In many cases punters can be both backers and layers on the same event at the same time.

Political betting – traditional bookmakers vs betting exchanges

An ongoing issue for political gamblers is that bookmakers are particularly wary about accepting bets in areas where their customers might have specialist or inside knowledge and therefore might be better able to assess the chances of an outcome than they are

Because the betting exchanges do not take any risks at all on the markets that are offered they are, in theory at least, able to be more ambitious opening up betting in areas where normal bookmakers would be reluctant to tread. Thus, in general elections, the exchanges are much more likely to have a wide range of constituency markets than the normal firms.

Another major feature during elections of all kind is that the betting exchanges can keep their markets open right up to the point that an outcome is known. So in the political area some of the biggest betting exchange activity takes place after the polls have closed while the counting is going on and where many punters might have inside knowledge. Standard bookmakers would simply not open themselves up to such a risk.

Using a betting exchange

After opening an account and making your first deposit you are in a position to start trading. It is wise for the rookie betting exchange punter to take things slowly at first. Moderate stakes until familiar with how the sites are constructed and how this form of betting operates. The betting exchanges have useful tutorials available so you can see for yourself how these markets behave.

Initially it is prudent to stick with betting for something rather than moving into the process of laying.

Price quotes

The first thing that might be unfamiliar is that betting exchanges quote prices differently. They operate on the decimal rather than the fractional odds system that most UK gamblers are familiar with. The prices with the main UK betting exchanges are quoted including your stake so that a conventional price of 2/1 appears as 3. So with a winning bet of £10 at 2/1 you receive back winnings of £20 plus your stake of £10. With the betting exchange a £10 winning bet at 3 produces a return to you of £30.

On the screen for the chosen market you will see a price and an amount that is available for you to bet at. If in the box (which with Betfair is shaded blue) the price level is 3 and there is a cash figure of, say, £50, then you simply place your bet by clicking on it. Up pops a trading box and you are asked to insert the amount you want to bet. You enter the required amount, £10 in this example, and then click OK. Once your transaction has taken place a confirmatory 'betting slip' appears with a transaction number on it.

You should notice that after completing your bet, the amount available at the price level of 3 will decline by £10 to £40 (from £50). In fast moving live sports markets a huge level of transactions are taking place all the time and the amount available and prices are changing by the second. Political markets, except on election nights when the results are coming through, tend to be much slower.

Now it might be that as you are placing your £10 bet at the price of 3 that others are doing the same and by the time you have completed the transaction other punters have beaten you to it and all the £50 that was available has gone. On the betting slip that you see, the bet you have placed is described as 'unmatched'.

Money will still have been taken from your account for this transaction but your bet is only operative if another punter is prepared to lay it at the 3 level. When this happens you will notice on the screen that the best backing price will have moved downwards, say, to 2.8 while your £10 bet will appear in the right hand pink box as being available to layers.

At this stage you have to decide whether you are prepared to bet at the reduced price level or leave your money on the board in the hope of a layer being prepared to accept it at the 3 level. To go for the reduced price, click on the 'My Bets' tab and change the price to 2.8. You then proceed to place the bet as before.

You might decide that you do not want to bet all at the lower price so all you have to do is click the cancel tab and your unmatched bet is taken off the market. Your account balance should be restored to what it was before.

Describing this might sound complicated, but in practice you should pick it up very quickly and it is worth persevering.

Why political gamblers prefer betting exchanges

Political betting is for many punters far more satisfactory on a betting exchange and, as we shall see, is much more flexible than a conventional bet with a bookmaker. Many political gamblers will not bet in any other way and will often choose the betting exchange route even on the rare occasions the prices are not as good.

Being able to both back and lay allows you to change your mind and even get your stake money back if you have been right about the way that the market is moving. It enables punters to operate for the short-term in long-term markets.

Case study – Betting exchange: cashing in your bet before the event has happened

Here is a good example of how a punter could have cashed in on the changing fortunes of the Conservative party in the UK, after its third election defeat in May 2005. Within a month a betting exchange had opened its next general election market and in June 2005 somebody placed a bet of £100 at the price of 2/1 (or 3, in the Betfair way of expressing odds). At that price a winning bet would produce a profit of £200.

By November 2006 sentiment had changed considerably and the Betfair lay price had tightened to 1.75. So our optimistic Conservative punter of June 2005 could then lay £100 at the new price and get his entire stake money back there and then. Remaining on the market would be a bet that would produce winnings of £125 if the Conservatives did end up as being the top party on seats. The bet would now be at entirely no risk to the punter. If the Conservatives did not end up as the winner he would still have all his stake money back. If they won he would pick up a profit of £125.

General election for Conservatives – bet and lay

Date	Bet	Price	Financial outcome
June 2005	The punter puts £100 on party to win most seats	3	£200 profit if correct, £100 loss if wrong
November 2006	The same punter lays £100 at the revised odds on Conservatives winning most seats	1.75	Overall £125 profit if correct. Punter gets stake back and risks no losses whatsoever if wrong

So what has happened here is that the punter has effectively sold part of his projected profits in exchange for all his money back.

This ability to both back and lay on the same proposition in long-term markets and get all or part of your stake money back is absolutely at the heart of betting exchange gambling and why people find it attractive. The experience is that once punters have done it successfully once or twice they become reluctant to bet any other way.

Betting exchange betting – the new possibilities

This facility to bet and lay opens up all sorts of possibilities to political gamblers who are confident of their ability to see the way the wind is blowing in a particular contest.

It also means that you can get out of bad bets on better terms than allowing your money to stay there until the outcome is known. So if our Conservative £100 punter had seen sentiment move against the party and the price had eased to 4 he could have laid at that level and got £66 of his original stake money back (without having to wait for the election and possibly losing all his money).

The great advantage is that it makes your betting that more flexible and you do not have to worry too much about locking your stake money up for years in long term markets (e.g. the winner of the next general election).

Because betting exchange prices are based on what actual punters, risking actual money are prepared to back and lay, they are usually a much better guide to how gamblers are seeing a market than the prices quoted by traditional bookmakers.

Betting exchange commission rates

The standard commission rate of most betting exchanges is 5% of your winnings in a market. Helpfully, commission is only paid on your net winnings on each market. This is particularly beneficial if you have multiple bets on a single market such as a party leadership election market. Some of your bets may win, some may lose, however you only pay commission on your *net* winnings. If your bets in a particular market amount to a net loss, you do not pay commission. Betfair and other betting exchanges offer customer incentive schemes. You can receive a discount off the standard Market Base Rate dependent on how much you bet. The more you bet, the larger the discount you receive.

Though this rate of commission may appear steep, generally speaking it compares favourably with the margins which traditional bookmakers seek.

Betting with an overseas betting exchange

Betting exchanges have become a very international business as others have tried to cash in on the phenomenal success of Betfair. One interesting firm that has developed very fast with a wide range of interesting political markets has been the Dublin-based, Intrade firm. This uses a pricing formula that is more common in the US than in the UK. Essentially what you see on their trading screens are odds presented in terms of their percentage implied probability. So a price of 50 equates to a 50% chance of that happening or 2 in the standard Betfair notation which is, of course, evens or 1/1 if expressed as a normal UK fractional price.

The range of markets
The main benefit of going to an overseas betting exchange is that the range of markets that are offered, particularly on US politics, is much wider than anything that is possible in the UK. Thus, for the mid-terms in November 2006, the Dublin firm had almost every single key race rather than just the big picture.

Intrade has also become well-known for its quirky markets, such as whether Osama Bin Laden will be captured or 'neutralised'. Whenever a leading US politician is in trouble Intrade will arrange betting on how long they will last in the job – something that Betfair used to do in the UK with British politicians before it decided that it ought to be respectable.

Currency risk

As well as the bet itself, an extra risk that you are taking with betting on any overseas market is that currency exchange rates might alter. Intrade operates exclusively in US dollars and you might find the value of your winnings has changed as the US dollar fluctuates in value.

Settlement risk

Another risk is what happens if, for whatever reason, your bet goes wrong? In the UK, the bookmakers have a well established procedure for dealing with disputes – the Independent Betting Arbitration Service. Although this is voluntary, it does give punters an extra safeguard. An argument over how, say, Intrade settled a complex political market, would leave you with little recourse.

As with a UK bookmaker your winnings on Intrade are tax-free.

Spread Betting

How spread betting started

The biggest betting innovation prior to the betting exchanges was the development of spread betting. This had its origins in the London financial markets in the mid-1970s when there was a ban on investors buying and selling gold. This prompted the innovative Stuart Wheeler, a barrister, to create, in effect, a bookmaking firm where investors could bet on the price of gold instead of, say, horses. The IG in IG Index stands for Investing in Gold.

This entrepreneurial approach led to Wheeler becoming very rich; at one stage he was the biggest donor to the Conservative party. His basic concept was to create a betting market which operated in a similar manner to trading in stocks and shares. By the early 1990s this had evolved into sport and then political markets.

There are now about a dozen spread betting firms operating in the UK and each follows fairly closely the original concept.

Spread betting – how it works

Spread betting is easiest to understand when the outcome is linked to a number such as how many seats a particular party will win at a general election.

Take as an example the morning of the general election day in May 2005, when the index firms were offering a spread of 182-186 on the number of Commons seats that the Conservatives would win. A punter approaches the firm with the belief that there will be more than 186 seats won by the party and buys at, say, £25 a seat at the stated level,186. The final outcome was 198 seats so the punter won the difference between what he had bought at and the actual result multiplied by the stake level.

A bet example

Conservative Party seat spread betting – 7am, general election day 2005

Spread price	182 – 186 seats
The bet	Buy at 186
Stake level	£25
Actual result	Conservatives 198 seats
Seats above the buy level	Actual minus Bet level = 198-186 = 12 seats
Calculating the profit	(Seat difference x Stake level) = 12 x £25 = £300

In this case a winning bet would have produced (198-186) x £25 = £300. If the final total of Conservative seats had been 180 then the punter would have lost (180-186) x £25 = -£150. A sell transaction is similar except made against the bottom value of the spread.

Spread betting – other political markets

The spread betting format works best when the outcome can be expressed in a numerical way and firms have often been highly creative in using this to establish interesting things to bet on.

After the May 2005 general election there was a huge amount of speculation on when exactly Tony Blair would step down. The betting exchanges and the traditional bookmakers offered markets which broke down possible leaving dates into different time segments and you chose which to go for. One spread betting firm, Cantor Spreadfair, had a different approach. This is how it explained its market:

> How many weeks will Tony Blair remain as Prime Minister during his third term in office? For the purposes of this market the week starting 9th May 2005 and ending 15th May 2005 is defined as week 1, the week starting 16th May 2005 as week 2, the week starting 23rd May 2005 as week 3, etc. The make up will always be a whole number, so it will be the same for each week, regardless of the particular day the term of office ends. If Tony Blair announces his resignation for a date in the future, but carries on as Prime Minister in the interim, then the market will be settled on his actual final day as Prime Minister, not the time of the announcement.

> Example: You sell Blair Weeks as PM for £10 at 60. Blair resigns on the 14th June 2005. The market is settled at week 6, and you win £10 stake times (60-6) = £540.

As it turned out Tony Blair remained as Prime Minister well into 2007, so the example punter above would not have made money.

Spread betting – the actual process

It is a feature of spread betting that you always see two prices quoted – the *buy* price which is the higher figure and the *sell* price which is the lower one.

Just like with betting exchange gambling, a punter is able to close a position out and consolidate profits or cut losses.

One of the great appeals of spread betting is that the more you are right, the more you win, although conversely the more that you are wrong the more you lose. It can be costly and anybody tempted into this form of betting needs to assess all the risks and their own financial situation.

The spread betting firms are always on the look out for innovative markets that fit in with their particular approach to betting. So during the Conservative leadership contest in 2005 there was active spread betting on "the age of the next Tory leader". Where there is no clear cut numerical outcome the firms often create their own, usually on the basis of giving a value of 25 to the winner of some event and 10 allocated to the second. A variation of this is termed *Binary Betting* by the spread betting firm IG Index. A series of possible outcomes to an event are listed and the prices relate to the percentage probability of the outcome happening with a buy and a sell spread.

Spread betting – how much cash do you need to put upfront?

A big issue for spread betting punters is how much cash they are asked to put up in stake money when they make their bets. This all depends on what sort of account you have. There are two approaches – you can usually have a deposit account or a credit account.

Deposit accounts

With deposit accounts the spread betting firm will usually agree with you a stop loss level with each bet and you will be asked to deposit enough money to cover that worst case scenario. So our Conservative punter above would probably have been required to provide upfront enough funds to deal with the party winning just 136 seats – 50 less than the agreed buy figure. At £25 a seat that would have been £1,250.

It used to be the case that the most you could win was the same as the most you could lose. That has changed and now most of the firms offer unlimited win on all bets meaning that if by any chance the Conservatives had won 50 more seats than the 186 in the bet then the punter would have made profits considerably in excess of £1,250.

Such accounts can be opened online, although you might have to wait for 24 hours before you can start betting.

Credit accounts

A second option, which is recommended for serious punters, is a credit account. With these you do not need to put any money upfront and there are no stop losses or stop wins.

To open a credit account, the firms request that you provide evidence that you have access to readily available funds of, say, five times the credit limit you require and you normally need to provide financial documentation to back this up. This cannot be opened online because you have to personally sign the application form. You also need to provide proof of identity, such as a photocopy of your passport, and an original recent utility bill.

The great advantage of such an account is that you can place bets without having to put any cash upfront.

The steps that spread betting firms go through before opening credit accounts are an indication of the risks that punters might face and this form of betting is only for the experienced and those who can afford to lose.

Case study – Pocketing your profits even though your choice was a loser

At precisely 9pm, BST, on Sunday May 29th, 2005 voting ended in the French referendum on whether the country should accept the draft new constitution for the European Union. A "Oui" would pave the way

CHOOSING THE RIGHT BETTING VEHICLE

for a similar referendum in the UK, which had been promised by Tony Blair a year earlier. This would also keep the issue of Britain's relationship with the EU very much alive and could impact on the Conservative party which has been split for more than a decade on Britain's relationship with the EU.

A possible candidate in the party's leadership race which was then under way was the former Chancellor, Kenneth Clarke, whose strong support of the EU had cost him the job four years earlier. If the French voted "Non" then the issue would be kicked into touch and Clark's chances would be enhanced.

Sitting in front of the TV I was waiting for the news of the French exit polls with my laptop on my knee, logged on to IG Index's Binary market on the Tory contest. Within a few seconds of the French result being announced I placed a spread bet on Clarke at the effective rate of about 11/1. At 9.06pm IG adjusted their Tory leader prices so that Clarke moved to the equivalent of about 6/1.

Over the next few days there was considerable speculation in the media about the new opportunity facing Clarke and his IG spread price started to soar. This enthusiasm was not shared by those posting on Tory web sites and a view was emerging that Clarke was simply unelectable within the party. The message coming out was that his distancing himself from the Euro-sceptic line, and his reluctance to moderate that position, meant, whatever the papers were saying, that he did not have a chance.

This sowed doubts in my mind about my bet and I decided to get out. So less than seven days after the French EU referendum result I sold my bet at the equivalent of 4.5/1 and pocketed a nice profit there and then.

Clarke, of course, went on to be defeated four months later when he failed to win the support of enough of his party's MPs to go on the short-list for the membership ballot. That did not affect my winnings on him.

Spread betting with other punters – the spread betting exchanges

Following in the wake of the success of the betting exchange, Betfair, the spread betting firm, Cantor Index, created SpreadFair where the same concept was applied to spread betting.

SpreadFair has been quite innovative in the number of political markets that it operates and because it is not taking the risk itself, it is able to make betting opportunities available where it does not have to monitor price movements on a regular basis.

Just like with standard betting exchange gambling, you see on the trading screen how much is available at different levels and you can either accept what is on the board or put something forward in the hope of attracting other punters.

Outside busy periods some of the Cantor Spreadfair markets have not attracted much interest and there have only been very small sums available to bet on. This lack of liquidity makes them less attractive.

Betting by credit card

All bookmakers and betting exchanges want to make it as easy as possible for you to bet and so most accept credit cards. Normally if you use the same bookmaker regularly your details will be stored and often all you have to quote are the card's three security numbers.

One problem with credit cards is that the bookmaker has to pay a merchant fee to the card company. The result is that some will not credit your account with the whole of your deposit. This is what happens with credit card deposits with Betfair.

Deposit amount using credit card	**£100**
Fee deducted by Betfair (1.5%)	£1.50
Amount creditied to your betting account	£98.50

The firm makes no deduction for deposits using debit cards issued by UK and Irish banks.

Using credit cards for making bets online or with a telephone bookmaker has now been made more difficult because of the actions of some of the card companies. Many of the ones which operate largely in the US have imposed restrictions on their accounts being used for betting even if by a customer based outside the US with a bookmaker who is also located outside. The result, in some cases such as cards from Citibank is that you simply cannot use them. Your only alternative is to get a card from a credit card company that will.

Extra charges on some credit cards
Another development has been a move by one or two card issuers to impose a fee on the user for betting related transactions. The card companies are arguing that they need to do this because of the extra credit risk element associated with those who gamble.

Use a debit card
So it could be that to use you credit card to bet you will be penalised by both the bookmaker and your card company. The best way to avoid fees from either the bookmaker or the card issuer is to use a debit card like Switch or Solo. So far these seem to be clear, but do not hold your breath.

Tax-free status of UK betting

Income and Capital gains tax
Betting in the UK has always been free of income and capital gains tax. If you win £500, from either betting on the horses or spread betting Tory seats at a general election, the tax man can't touch your winnings – you keep the lot and you do not have to declare them on your income tax return.

Betting duty

On October 6th 2001 a new taxation regime for gambling in the UK came into force abolishing the betting duty which had led bookmakers to impose the 9 per cent deduction that they charged punters. The general *betting duty*, as it was known, had been in place for 35 years. Up until that date punters had to decide whether or not to pay the tax upfront with their stake or have it deducted from any winnings. Whichever way, it made betting less economic.

The change followed a move by the Treasury to "bring the UK betting industry back home" after many of the big names in the industry had set up off-shore operations, mainly in Gibraltar, to avoid the tax. As part of the agreement a new tax of 15% of their gross profits was imposed on bookmakers.

The effect was to make betting in the UK that much more attractive and this, together with the rise of the internet and the betting exchanges, and the light regulatory touch, has led to the huge expansion in the industry.

This means that punters now pay no tax on their stake; and, as before, they receive 100% of their profits.

**Betting Tactics
UK General Elections**

3
Betting Tactics
UK General Elections

Overview

General elections are like the Football World Cup for those who get pleasure trying to predict and bet on political outcomes. They are the big events that come along every four years or so. And like the football aficionados who can talk about little else, those with a passion for politics put a huge amount of effort into speculating how voters will behave during those fifteen hours when the polling stations are open on Election Day. The groups – party activists, punters, journalists, academics, pollsters, as well as politicians themselves – judge almost every event and development in terms of its possible electoral impact. Also like football, it has to be said, there are some women participants but the vast majority are male.

These are people who scrutinise each single policy development, opinion poll or the results of minor council by-elections, for signs that they can then extrapolate in terms of what will happen 'next time'. They have also got good detailed knowledge about what is happening in particular seats.

The ongoing obsession amongst some with the next general election often spills out into the way politics is reported in influential parts of the media. Listen to BBC Radio 4's flagship Today programme and barely a week goes by without some reference to the "next general election", however far ahead that might be. So a report on NHS reorganisation soon moves away from the health care issues into a discussion of its impact on MPs in marginal constituencies!

The perpetual general election campaign

It is as though we are in a perpetual general election campaign and this is seen in the betting. Less than a week after the May 5th 2005 general election, active betting started on the next one. The opening price on Labour was about 3/5 – punters putting £50 on in May 2005 could look forward, at best, to their stake back and a profit of just £30.

Quite who is betting on these long-term markets at such prices is not clear. They would almost certainly be better off putting their money in the building society for four years, where there would be no risk. Clearly some punters take pleasure in making a wining bet several years ahead.

In 2005, spurred on by the extraordinary amount of betting six months earlier in the White House race of 2004, the bookmakers in all sections of the market took the general election very seriously indeed. There was a bigger range of betting markets available than ever before even though, unlike the US, the overall result was never really in doubt. In spite of that the bookmakers came up with a plethora of things to tempt political punters to bet on.

Before we look at the specific betting options, it is important to examine how the electoral system operates when it comes to converting votes cast for a party into the number of MPs it is likely to get. This is central to so many betting decisions.

How the electoral system helps Labour

By far the biggest issue in the main 'who will win' betting is projecting suggested vote shares into the number of Commons seats that each party will end up with. Anybody risking money on a UK general election other than for a bit of fun should have an awareness of the issues involved and the predictions that show that a Labour deficit on votes will not necessarily carry over into a Labour deficit on seats.

This is because for a whole host of reasons the electoral system has traditionally worked better for Labour than the Conservatives or the Liberal Democrats.

The scale of what happened in 2005 is best represented by the aggregated results in the 529 English seats.

Party	Votes	Seats	Vote per seat
Conservatives	8,114,979	194	41,829
Labour	8,050,366	286	24,148
Lib. Democrats	5,201,129	47	110,662

Some of this distortion will be removed by the boundary changes that come into effect during 2007. But even with these, Martin Baxter (Cambridge University and now City mathematician), has calculated for his Electoral Calculus website that if Labour and the Conservatives were level on votes then Labour would have 110 more MPs and still maintain a Commons majority.

In February 2007 two academics from the University of Plymouth, Colin Rallings and Michael Thrasher, produced the following benchmarks for relating vote shares to seats at the following general election, assuming there is a uniform national swing in each constituency.

Swing	Outcome
Any swing to Labour	Increased Labour majority in the House of Commons
A swing to the Conservatives of up to 1.56%	Labour returned to power but with a smaller majority
A swing of between 1.56% to 4.39% from Labour to the Conservatives	A hung parliament with Labour having the most seats
A swing of between 4.39% to 6.1 from Labour to the Conservatives	A hung parliament with the Conservatives having the most seats
A swing of greater than 6.1 from Labour to the Conservatives	A Conservative overall majority

These are benchmarks and do not take into account the performance of the Liberal Democrats and other parties.

There are three main reasons for why the hurdles seem to be so high for the Conservatives:

1. The system of resolving boundaries continues to favour Labour, particularly in Wales which based on its population should have 32 seats but in fact gets 40.

2. Differential turnout. In seats where Labour has a big majority or where it is so far behind that the party has no chance of winning then its supporters are much less likely to actually vote. Conservative voters are much more likely than Labour ones to turn out where it does not matter thus piling extra votes onto the national totals without having an impact on seat numbers.

3. The experience of recent elections is that Labour supporters are much more likely to switch to the Liberal Democrats to impede the Conservatives, than Tory supporters are prepared to do when they are in third place. There has also been a high level of Liberal Democrat to Labour switching in the past three general elections.

Calculating seat totals from projected vote shares

A substantial amount of betting activity at general elections is on how many seats each party will end up with, so those investing in the various seat markets need to get a good projection of how many Commons seats a particular set of vote shares would produce.

Firstly it should be recognised that there is no fail-safe way of tapping some numbers into a computer which will then give you an accurate prediction of how many MPs the parties would get for those vote shares. In fact the two most widely available online calculators employ very different mathematical approaches, and can in certain instances come out with very different seat numbers.

- www.electoralcalculus.co.uk: the excellent Electoral Calculus website, run by Martin Baxter (referred to above),

- www.ukpollingreport.co.uk: the also excellent, and comprehensive, UK Polling Report web site run by Anthony Wells.

I visit both the above sites daily.

Uniform National Swing
The big division is on how the two calculate what is known as the *Uniform National Swing*.

The Baxter approach is based broadly on the proportionality of the swing; Wells follows the traditional route of simply applying the same points change in vote shares to every seat. The division is best illustrated with parties who, like the Liberal Democrats in January 2007, were seeing their poll shares decline.

If the polls show that the party has lost a third of its vote since the general election (22.7% down to 15%) then Baxter will knock a third off their share in each seat and then make a calculation. The Wells approach would be to knock off, in this case, seven and a bit points in each seat. So in a seat where the LDs got 45% at the last election Baxter would reduce that to 30% while Wells has it at 38%. This can produce massive differences in seat projections.

To add to the complication it is important to stress that both have factored in the effect of the 2007 boundary changes. Their seat predictions are based on projections of how those constituencies would have gone with the new boundaries.

So which system is best – Wells or Baxter?

The answer is inconclusive. Baxter has tested the data from both approaches from previous elections and found no appreciable differences except at the 1997 general election when, of course, there was a massive swing to Labour. Both approaches to calculating seats underestimated how many Tony Blair's party would pick up. According to Martin Baxter, who back tested his approach, the proportional model did better by eight seats.

If a general election looks set to be a step change, you should treat the calculators with an extra degree of scepticism.

The best strategy, particularly for spread betting on Common seats with the financial risk that entails, is to run both models and look through the seats changing hands so you can draw your own conclusions.

A particular issue is what happens to the Liberal Democrats which tend to buck a lot of trends when it comes to national swings. The party has a long history of holding onto seats that the national swing suggested they should lose. You need to make your own decisions!

With Labour-Conservative marginals it tends to be a lot more straight-forward.

General elections – the different markets

As mentioned before, there are many different ways of betting on a general election. Some of the more popular markets are:

1. Which party will win most seats?

2. How many seats for each party?

3. Individual constituency outcomes

4. Party shares

5. Turnout

6. Total of women MPs

7. Number of seats changing hands

8. The first seat to declare

These are explained in more detail below.

1. Which party will win most seats?

This is usually described as the 'main' market and is the first one to be opened after the previous election. It is important to note that this is not on the overall outcome, such as one party having enough MPs to form a majority or for no single party to have overall control – a 'hung parliament'. The markets are simply about which party will end up with the most seats. Clearly the prices are usually pretty tight and the week-by-week movements are very much driven by the opinion polls.

In the final few days of a general election campaign, many gamblers who are not political specialists come into this market and tend to follow the favourite. Two days before the 2005 general election, William Hill reported that they had laid a bet from a woman punter of £72,000 at just 1/40 that Tony Blair's party would win most seats. Her winnings were less than £2,000 yet that is not a bad return for locking up the cash for a couple of days on what could only have been a certainty. It would take a lot longer leaving that sum in the building society to get so much interest and betting winnings are, of course, completely free of tax.

The lesson here is that if you want to back a strong favourite in such a market then get it on early. If this woman had placed the same bet just nine weeks earlier she should could have got odds of 1/8 and a profit of £9,000 on her investment.

By the same logic if you want to bet on a party that is not the strong favourite in such a market then wait till polling day itself. You will get substantially better prices.

Another winning party type bet is on the actual outcome – "A Labour majority, a Tory majority or a Hung Parliament?"

Sample prices from Betfair on the Overall Majority market (March 20 2007)

Next General Election - Overall Majority						Options ▶
Change: Express view | Full view				Matched: GBP 47,932		Refresh
Selections: (4)	102.6%		Back	Lay		99.8%
No Overall Majority	2.38 £47	2.4 £34	2.42 £7	2.44 £7	2.46 £22	2.48 £6
Conservative Majority	2.9 £25	2.92 £20	2.94 £16	3.05 £55	3.1 £150	3.15 £26
Labour Majority	3.75 £25	3.8 £51	3.85 £15	4 £13	4.1 £70	4.2 £100
Any Other Party Majority	70 £16	75 £2	80 £2	95 £4	100 £15	250 £25

2. How many seats for each party?

There are two main forms of activity here – the seat number markets with the traditional bookmakers and the betting exchanges and spread betting on the number of Commons seats. For the former the bookmakers list a series of options on the number of seats in 10, 15 or 20 seat segments. A price is attached to each and you make your choice.

The frustrating feature of having to choose a specific segment is that there are no prizes if you are nearly right. The odds tend to be in line with the projections that are made from poll figures on how many Commons seats parties will end up with based on the latest poll figures.

The gambling areas that I find appealing and where I have made and, it has to be said, lost a lot of money over the years are the Commons seats spread betting markets. As explained in Chapter 2 here you buy and sell seat numbers at a particular level and your winnings and losses are determined by the difference between the actual result and the price you invested at multiplied by your cash value per seat.

This is the betting area for serious gamblers particularly those ready to risk substantial amounts. In the final days of a campaign some very big money comes onto the market. One punter, with two days to go in the 2005 election bought Labour on the overall majority spread market at £2000 a seat above 84 seats.

A significant part of my profits on other betting markets at the 2005 general election was frittered away in one unwise Commons seat spread bet made just four hours before the polls closed. I got carried away with reports of the Liberal Democrats progress and bought several hundred pounds a seat at 67. The party finished up with 62 seats. Ouch!

3. Individual Constituency outcomes

A big growth betting area at the 2005 general election was on the results in individual constituencies. By the week of polling day there were well over 150 separate possibilities covering just about all the marginal seats where big battles were going on. A lot of the money was being placed by activists and others who were working on those campaigns. They, of course, had a much clearer view of what was happening and the chance to make a profit by putting a bet on was very tempting.

These days it has become much harder to assess how a campaign is going in a local seat. Yes, you have the broad national swing calculated from the opinion polls but each constituency is very different. Also the Conservatives and Labour have established national direct marketing operations which were working very actively, using the phone and bespoke direct mail, on voters in the key seats.

This 'under the radar' campaigning is not obviously visible, making judgements about how specific local campaigns are going that much harder. Even seeing lots of posters in voters' windows for one party is less of an indication than it was.

Adding to the complication for the punter is postal voting. You get reports on how many have been applied for in a particular seat and it is easy to assume that those are in the bag for the party organisations that persuaded the voters to put applications in. Yet getting people on the postal vote list is only half the battle. You also have to ensure that they do actually vote. This is being made harder by clampdowns caused by one or two major vote fraud cases.

Actually using a postal vote is quite a challenge for those who have them, involving getting a witness and putting everything into the right envelopes. To assist, local party officers usually call on people on their postal vote list when they know the packages have been delivered. Often it is they who act as the witness. In the aftermath of the voter fraud cases this practice is frowned upon and many volunteer workers are reluctant to do this job.

The result in many seats in 2005 was a relatively low turnout amongst those who had gone to all the trouble in the first place to apply for them. All this makes calling individual constituencies that much harder.

The best sources of information about how a campaign is going within an individual seat are the local party organisations and this often filters out. But you really have to judge carefully the reliability of the source of any information you get and make your betting judgements accordingly. Unless you have good information it is best to follow the betting in a local seat rather than to lead it.

4. Party shares

An area where a bit of specialist knowledge comes in handy is on the party shares markets, which are usually offered by the spread betting firms. What percentage of the popular vote will Labour, the Conservatives etc get? The small print will show that bookmakers usually operate this on an all-UK basis and not the England, Scotland and Wales format that is how opinion polls are carried out.

Because a lot of punters are probably not aware of this difference, they tend to be influenced by the surveys and party shares that come out almost every day during a general election. This has an effect of forcing the spread price up and the best strategy is always to look for sell situations when spread betting. Thus if you think that the Conservatives are doing well then it is less risky to sell Labour than buy your chosen party.

A few days before the May 2005 general election day I was able to sell Labour at 37.5% for a four figure sum per percentage point. The all-UK figure at the close was just over 35% - an outcome that more than made up for my sudden rush of blood to the head on the number of Liberal Democrats seats.

5. Turnout

I have a theory that in the second week of every general election campaign the media narrative always moves from the excitement of the party launches to "nothing seems to be happening". So a story begins to gather momentum that there will be "massive voter apathy". People are interviewed in the street saying that the whole business is a big turnoff and a poll will come out that seems to suggest that the turnout will reach a record low.

This is the time to bet on the turnout rising. There are two reasons: a massive amount of work has been going on to "clean up" the electoral register so that even if vote levels stay the same there will appear to be an increase. Secondly, as the frenzy steps up in the final few days interest does increase and more people than you think will start to get interested.

Turnout bets are usually available from all the different forms of bookmakers.

6. Total of women MPs

This is a market where a bit of good research can put you into a position to make a fairly accurate prediction. Use the UK Polling Report site and other to track the seats and work out the number. It generally runs fairly closely to the uniform national swing but you are dealing with a smaller overall total.

There is some evidence that women voters tend to be more inclined, on the margins, to vote for another woman but that men do not care that much either way.

7. Number of seats changing hands

This is an odd market and followed the 2001 general election when the number of seats changing hands touched a record low. Here the calculation you should make is more than just seat changes predicted by the party swings. There will be seats that go either way with, say, the Liberal Democrats picking up some constituencies from the Conservatives, but also losing them. If you have predicted a high figure then the more of this that goes on the better.

You will be helped as well by the fact that a seat changing hands will also include those where the outgoing MPs have switched allegiances during the previous parliament. If this, as usually happens, returns to what it was at the general election before, then this adds to the overall total of changes.

In 2005 there was quite a lot of money to be made by spread betting on these markets. My guess is that the bookmakers will not get stung to the same extent in future general elections.

8. The first seat to declare

This is usually a fun betting market and the standard rule was: always put your money on Sunderland South. Amazingly, for several general elections, they have got the ballot boxes to the central counting hall and had everything sorted and counted in time for a declaration by 10.45pm at the latest. Who knows how they do it but every four years or so Sunderland gets its 15 minutes of fame! Following the 2007 boundary changes Sunderland South is no more and we now just have a Sunderland Central seat. Will this make any difference? I doubt it – keep putting your money on Sunderland.

Betting Tactics
Other Major Markets

4
Betting Tactics
Other Major Markets

Party Leadership Contests

Overview

As the success of TV programmes like "Big Brother" has shown, large sections of the public love the opportunity to vote, and sometimes to bet, in elections on people whose personalities they think they have come to know and understand through the wall-to-wall coverage.

So it is in political betting. Apart from a main general election, there is nothing that quite fires up the imagination of political punters so much as a battle between individuals for the leadership of a party. So much is at stake for the contestants that usually these have a gladiatorial feel about them. Certainly that is how the media likes to portray them.

Ever since the Tory leadership battle in front of the TV cameras after the Profumo affair in 1963, these have always attracted wide coverage because the media bosses know that their audiences are much more interested in a clash between ambitious personalities and egos than the minutiae of policies.

There is something that is compulsive and compelling about contestants like David Davis and David Cameron in the 2005 Tory election, being prepared to go on Woman's Hour on Radio 4 and be questioned about what sort of underpants they wear. In what other area of public life would that happen? A few months later there was the 2006 Liberal Democrat race, which to watch was awful, yet at the same time completely absorbing, as one candidate after another saw their private life being torn to shreds by the tabloids. Britain's third party rarely sees so much coverage.

What does it say about politicians like this that they are prepared to risk such public humiliation in order to be elected to a top job? It is those character features that make them stand apart from ordinary people and lesser politicians, and why such contests are almost always big betting events. In each of these fights, the gambling interest is enormous.

Unlike "Big Brother", of course, it is not the mass television audience that decides – the parties all have elaborate election rules. For the punter wanting to come out of such an election as a winner the first step is to understand how the party election processes work and the dynamics of the different constituencies that decide the fate of those who put themselves forward. Each party works differently and each has followed very different approaches.

The introduction of mass membership ballots

A dimension that has really put the spark into these contests has been the introduction in all three main parties of mass membership ballots as part of the leadership electoral process. The fact that hundreds of thousands of individuals can be part of the election has made the broadcasters, in particular, sit up. It is now hard to imagine a contest without the televised leadership debates and big set-piece interviews with the contestants.

The Jeremy Paxman grilling on BBC2's Newsnight programme has almost become part of the official process, and with the Tory and Liberal Democrat leadership battles of 2005 and 2006 were major betting events in themselves.

With Labour, before their 1993 contest, and the Tories before 2001, the decisions were all in the hands of MPs. Of course there was a great media interest but the extra element of mass voting made them into more interesting spectacles for punters. A smart Westminster correspondent can soon get a good feel of how a party's MPs are thinking. With a mass ballot nobody can know for sure.

The Liberal Democrats, of course, have always selected their leaders in this way but they, too, have benefited from the changes in the two main parties.

Conservatives

History

Whether the Tories are in government or in opposition, battles for the leadership of the party always seem to attract a lot of interest and a lot of betting. It was the Tories, it will be recalled, who took the pioneering decision in 1975 to elect a woman, something that none of the other parties have ever got close to doing.

For Tory contests have always seemed to throw up surprises. The obvious candidate never seems to make it. Who would have guessed that at the end of the Margaret Thatcher era in 1990 that it would be the relatively unknown John Major, rather than the charismatic Michael Heseltine, who would end up victorious and lead the party to a fourth general election victory and serve seven years at Number 10?

When Major stepped down after the Labour landslide in 1997, few predicted that the young William Hague would beat off heavyweights like Ken Clarke and Michael Howard for the job.

Four years later, after a second disastrous general election defeat, everything seemed set for Michael Portillo to take over in the contest that followed William Hague's resignation. Yet such was the way the election process operated he did not make the final that everybody assumed would happen – Portillo against Ken Clarke. He did not get onto the final short-list of two that went to the mass membership ballot.

The party chose instead Iain Duncan Smith, who was almost unknown outside the Westminster village and was not the choice of the parliamentary party.

Then in 2005 the Conservatives surprised us again. The early front-runner and odds-on favourite, who had won the public backing of the largest number of Tory MPs, the Shadow Home Secretary, David Davis, suddenly saw his leadership chances fall away during his party conference in Blackpool. He became the main casualty of a well planned campaign by the youthful but relatively unknown ex-PR man, David Cameron, who seemed to come from nowhere to win the support of the conference and then the mass membership to take the crown.

All of these races had many different stages and a massive amount of betting. Those who read them right were able to make a lot money.

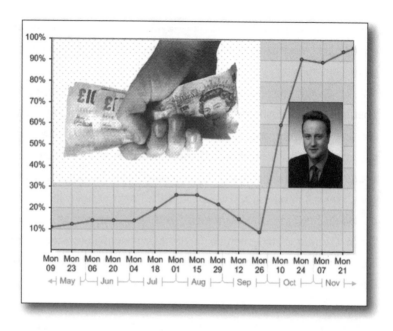

Above can be seen how the betting markets reflected the emergence of David Cameron during the 2005 Conservative leadership contest. The chart shows changing assessments of his implied probability of winning, based on the best betting prices that were available at the time.

The election process

The rules for Conservative leadership contests have changed substantially since Sir Alec Douglas-Home became Prime Minister in 1963, after the 'men in grey suits' held informal, secret consultations and made a recommendation to the Queen.

The latest version was introduced by William Hague after his election in 1997. The idea is that both the party's MPs and the membership should have a big say, with the former group deciding the two names that should be put forward to the party membership in a mass ballot.

All of this adds to the betting interest because each stage sees the possibility of a fresh turn. The great unknown is that although candidates might be doing well in the polls, and be popular amongst the membership, their fellow MPs still have the power to stop them going to the national ballot – as happened with Michael Portillo in 2001.

So the process starts at Westminster with a series of ballots amongst the party's MPs on which of their colleagues should go forward to the membership ballot. In 2005 it took three rounds at Westminster before David Davis and David Cameron became the short-list of two to go forward. The outcome of the membership ballot is the only one that counts.

Betting tactics
What has become the golden rule in Tory leadership contests is that whoever is the early front runner does not make it. This has happened so often, even though there are stages when the favourite, like David Davis in 2005, looks unassailable. So the top tip for punters is to always lay a firm early favourite.

There is now a second golden rule in Tory contests. The internet pollster YouGov has built up such an amazing record predicting the result of the membership ballots with its surveys of Tory party members that you should always follow what these polls report. In 2001 the firm got the percentage of the vote that Iain Duncan Smith would get against Ken Clarke right to within one percent. Amazingly, it followed this up four years later by predicting the David Cameron election with the same level of accuracy.

The third golden rule is not to go overboard with support for any one candidate, until it is clear that they are going to get through to the final ballot. I lost a lot of money on Michael Portillo in 2001 by not following this rule.

Punters have to be very careful during these elections to read the detail of the polls. What matters is support amongst party members who are able to vote in the election. Occasionally surveys come out reporting what people of all parties think about the race, or what Tory supporters want. The latter are not members and, for punters, their views are not relevant.

Labour

History

Labour has had a long history of its leadership contests being seen both internally and externally as a battle between left and right. There is almost always an ideological dimension, where the key issue has been who would be the standard bearer for the left and who would take on the same role for the right.

These left-right battles have also often been the focus for contests for the deputy leadership, which also attracts betting interest.

For decades the decision on who would be the leader was left solely in the hands of the Parliamentary Labour Party.

Only once in the party's history until 2007 has Labour had to choose a new leader while in government. That was in 1976, after the shock resignation of Harold Wilson. Five leading figures put their hats into the ring and James Callaghan came out on top. It was always said that Wilson had tipped him off about his intentions which gave him a head start when the election, which was then restricted to MPs, actually started.

In 1979 Callaghan lost to Margaret Thatcher's Tories, and a big ideological battle began within the Labour party. The left-winger, Michael Foot, beat Denis Healey in the MPs ballot and went on to lose disastrously in the 1983 general election. His election manifesto was described as "the longest suicide note in history".

Foot's replacement was Neil Kinnock, who beat Roy Hattersley who was seen to represent the right. Kinnock went on to prepare the ground for some of the reforms the party needed if, in the eyes of many, it was ever to gain power.

None of these leadership elections were seen as being close and in each case the betting favourite came out on top. By 1993 when John Smith beat Bryan Gould the party had in place a new electoral structure that gave members a say for the first time. This was reformed ahead of the 1994 contest that was caused by John Smith's death. Tony Blair was elected in the first of the new style arrangements.

The election process

The election is decided by an electoral college made up of three equal elements: the party's MPs, the party membership, and those who belong to what are termed 'affiliated organisations' (which means mostly the trade unions). The old days of the trade union block vote are now over and this section of the ballot is decided by the postal votes of individual members of the organisations which, in the case of a trade union, is restricted to those paying the political levy.

Multiple voting is allowed, so MPs can vote in the parliamentary party part of the electoral college, as individual members in their own constituencies, and in as many of the ballots amongst the affiliated organisations that they are members of. During the 1994 election that saw Tony Blair take the leadership one MP reported that he had seven separate votes.

Clearly their votes as an MP are the most valuable. Somebody worked out that one Labour MP has the same impact on the outcome of the election as 500 individual party members and 2,777 trade unionists.

To get on the ballot in the first place, an MP needs to have the support of 12.5% of the Parliamentary Labour Party, which in 2007 meant 45 different supporters. Just to get on the ballot was a tall order for all but the firm favourite.

Betting tactics

The real challenge here is trying to work out what is going on in each of the three prongs of the electoral college. Is it right to assume that they will all be moving in the same direction? That might not be the case.

Punters are helped by the internet pollster, YouGov, which has the capability of testing opinion amongst both Labour members and those in trade unions who are able to vote in their mass ballots. With MPs the political correspondents are usually able to give reasonable estimates.

By the start of 2007, however, this election system had only been used once – thirteen years earlier when Labour was in opposition and when Tony Blair was the obvious front-runner. While a big question remains about whether union leaders have any impact on the votes of their members, it does appear that a bet on the favourite is the right strategy.

The challenge of getting enough nominations looks quite daunting. Certainly it would be very difficult for outsiders to find 44 other MPs to sign the nomination forms.

Looking back over Labour's previous leadership elections the job, almost invariably, has gone to the front-runner.

Labour leadership betting – Gordon Brown price May 2005 – March 2007

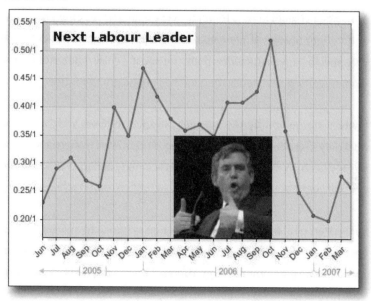

Liberal Democrats

History

Established in its current form in 1987, the Liberal Democrats have only had three leadership elections – all of them involving membership ballots and using the single transferable vote system. After all, they cannot press for proportional representation nationally and not employ it within the party!

The form book for the party suggests that it is usually the most well-known candidate who gets elected. This is not altogether surprising, it is always a challenge for a third party to command reasonable air-time and column inches while the two big boys are battling it out. The prospect of anybody other than the most senior spokesmen and women getting any media attention has been very low indeed.

So the first contest in 1987 was won by Paddy Ashdown; and the second by Charles Kennedy who had built up quite a high name recognition factor due to his regular appearances on comedy and quiz programmes on radio and TV.

When Kennedy had to step down in January 2006, the party got more coverage for the ensuing contest than it had ever seen before. This was partly because its contingent of MPs had reached 62 in the preceding general election, and precedents for coverage had been set with the Tory contest a month or so earlier on how the broadcasters would cover it.

It would have been courting considerable criticism if the BBC, say, had not had a televised debate between the contestants, as had been held for the Tories. On top of this, there was the heavy coverage of the private lives of two of the early declared runners, and the Lib-Dem exceptional victory – while still leaderless – in the Dunfermline by-election.

The 2006 contest was notable for a very determined attempt by an MP who had been in the Commons for less than a year, Chris Huhne. He became the betting favourite for a time, and there were suggestions that somebody was backing him heavily in order to influence the election. This is covered elsewhere in the book.

Prices on Chris Huhne in the Lib-Dem leadership contest, 2006

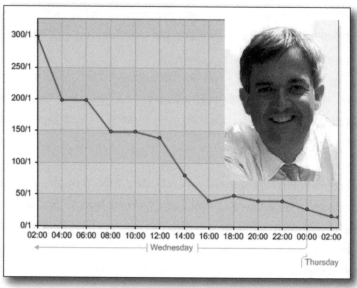

The chart shows the Liberal Democrat leadership betting markets from January 10-12th, 2006, when Chris Huhne moved from being a 300/1 outsider to a serious contender within a very short time. Those who got on Huhne at the big prices were able to make a lot of money laying their position when Hune became favourite for a time.

The election process

The Liberal Democrats leadership election process is simple and easy to understand. To get on the ballot a candidate needs the nominations of 10% of the parliamentary party. While this might be seen to be a problem, a number of party MPs in 2006 declared that they were ready to nominate more than one candidate – a device which clearly got round the 10% rule that had only been introduced four months earlier.

This then goes out to a postal ballot of the membership who vote using the single transferable vote system.

Betting tactics

The internet pollster, YouGov, carried out surveys during the 2006 election, but did not achieve the same level of accuracy as it had with the Tories. The pollster did, however, suggest very early on that one of the contenders, Simon Hughes, did not stand much of a chance – which proved to be the case. So take YouGov quite seriously, but if the poll is showing the election as a close thing go for the candidate who has the highest public profile.

It is very hard for most candidates to build up enough name recognition, amongst what are described as the party's 'arm-chair members', to stand any chance at all.

Betting on the 2006 Liberal Democrat leadership contest

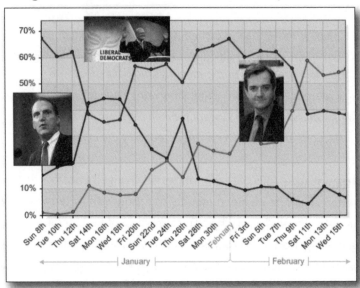

The chart shows the changing implied probabilities (based on the best betting prices at the time) of victory as the campaign progressed.

Westminster By-Elections

It used to be that parliamentary by-elections were major events on the British electoral calendar. All the papers posted reporters in the constituencies for large parts of the campaigns – they attracted a massive amount of media coverage and the betting was big. For some reason, they do not attract the interest they once did and it is hard to work out why.

This is what the *Guardian* political writer, Michael White, wrote in 2004–

> By- elections are not the thriving political industry they used to be. No more rowdy public meetings, no daily press conferences where the candidates were made to squirm by the BBC's legendary Vincent Hannah. There are not many by-elections anyway. MPs no longer routinely die in harness.

The point about MPs' life expectancies has changed a bit since that was written. The first eighteen months of Labour's third term saw five contests, almost all of which had great political interest for the main two parties. Yet apart from coverage of the results and the aftermath there was not the same scale of media interest as there was in the past.

Because the betting is usually prompted by the public interest there have been very weak markets on by-elections and therefore a lack of liquidity. In two cases following the 2005 general election the betting markets got the outcomes wrong.

Betting On The Opinion Polls

De-linking political betting from elections

A big challenge for the bookmaker firms has been to try to cash in on the growing interest in political betting by creating regular markets that are not linked to elections – some of which can be years ahead.

Many punters like the notion of being able to bet on something today that will be resolved by the weekend at the latest.

The Dublin-based Intrade company offers regular markets on the approval ratings of the US President, based on a range of different surveys and as calculated by a leading political web-site.

The YouGov BrandIndex markets

BrandIndex betting prices – January 24th 2007

Price Finder					
Politics ▼	YouGov Politicians' Popularity ▼		Week ending 26 Jar		
Based on YouGov Brand Index +100. Results at www.yougov.co.uk. Book closes Friday 15.00					
Market		Period	Sell	Buy	So Far
BET	Tony Blair Popularity	i JAN-07	61.3	61.8	
BET	Gordon Brown Popularity	i JAN-07	67.5	68	
BET	John Reid Popularity	i JAN-07	75	75.5	
BET	Jack Straw Popularity	i JAN-07	73.3	73.8	
BET	Alan Johnson Popularity	i JAN-07	83.8	84.3	
BET	Patricia Hewitt Popularity	i JAN-07	68.3	68.8	
BET	Boris Johnson Popularity	i JAN-07	92.5	93	
BET	Hilary Benn Popularity	i JAN-07	90.5	91	
BET	David Cameron Popularity	i JAN-07	90.3	90.8	
BET	William Hague Popularity	i JAN-07	95.3	95.8	

In January 2007 the spread betting firm IG Index, teamed up with the internet pollster, YouGov, to open a new weekly market based on how the reputations of leading politicians move in the pollster's BrandIndex ratings.

Each week more than 11,000 on the pollster's panel complete surveys asking them to rate a range of different brands. In addition, politicians names are mentioned and people are asked to tick boxes against those they feel positively about and those where they have a negative view. For the betting market YouGov is subtracting the negative data from the positive and adding 100 to create a form of index.

The market is opened on Monday mornings and settled on what has happened by Friday. I am assured that strict measures are being taken so that the data cannot be accessed by anybody while betting is taking place.

BrandIndex tactics

What seems to drive an individual politician's BrandIndex rating is how much they have been in the news during the week of the market. This seems to affect the positive side of the rating. The negative number seems to be much less variable.

My approach, after the first few weeks, was to wait until the Friday afternoon, a couple of hours before market closes, and then take a view on who has been in the news most in the previous seven days.

Regular gamblers in this form of betting need to maintain their own spreadsheet, updating it each week, so they can see for themselves how different names are moving.

Betting Tactics
Following the Betting

5
Betting Tactics
Following the Betting

Overview

It is often thought that a common source for information about what is going on in an event on which people are gambling is the betting itself. Prices move up and down all the time and there is a widespread view that it is sometimes possible from observing the weight of money going one way or another to come to a view that will allow profitable bets to be made.

Be warned, as the case studies that follow show, this can be dangerous. Punters might be following other punters who they think are in the know – in which case the market becomes circular, and totally wrong.

Another danger is that, for those closely involved, politics is a very serious business, and in the eyes of many participants almost everything is justifiable in order to win an election. Occasionally there have been attempts to manipulate betting odds in order to show that some person or party is seen as having a greater chance of success. What better than to have your man or woman described as (in that term so loved by journalists) – "the bookies' favourite"? This can help to build up credibility and is seen as such a powerful tool that practitioners often try to manipulate things so that their cause is looking good. But as we discuss later, this should be seen as an opportunity and not a threat.

Following the betting case studies

Below are three separate examples of how punters who followed the betting could, and did, use information that helped enhance their betting positions, and how some lost out badly.

In one case the betting pattern would have led those who followed to a profit; in another it led those who went against it to profit and in a third the betting movements were caused by other punters thinking they were following those "in the know", but were wrong.

Case study – Dunfermline by-election, February 2006

The lesson here: it can be dangerous following the betting. Below are comments posted on the Politicalbetting web site, as punters were waiting for the Dunfermline by-election result to come in at just after midnight on the morning of February 10th 2006. The comments convey the drama and the uncertainty as a result is about to be declared and show huge fluctuations in the betting.

It will be recalled that this seat had been held easily by Labour in the 2005 general election, and that it took place bang in the middle of the race for the leadership of the Liberal Democrats.

Labour had gone into the contest as very strong favourite and had retained that status almost up to the end. This is how the final 25 minutes looked to gamblers. It serves as a salutary warning to all who think they can make money following the betting on such occasions.

News 24 – Lib Dems look like they've won according to Curtice.
ukpl at 12:08 am

From BBC – 'Lib Dems may have done it'
T at 12:08 am

Money available on Lib Dems betfair at 2.0 – £100 if you want it!
UKP at 12:09 am

Gone now.
UKP at 12:10 am

Sky News – 'village vote' may win it for Labour. VERY close.
Tim at 12:10 am

Lib Dems narrow favourite on Betfair. Update... recount possible... "Labour glum". HEALTH warning still counting!
Jack W at 12:15 am

Labour favourites again on Betfair
C at 12:23 am

I will have to rely on Wireless Four as usual. Their man at the count talks of Labour holding on, but only just.
AC at 12:24 am

Exactly matched on 1.8 now...
C at 12:24 am

Looks like Labour.
ML 2006 at 12:27 am

Betfair indicating a Labour hold. I'm afraid
SW at 12:28 am

There's money to be had on Betfair at 1.2 if Labour have won -
C at 12:29 am

Really poor show from the news channels here.
UKP at 12:30 am

LD won
A at 12:32 am

Bloody hell!
ST 2006 at 12:33 am

You can't back the Lib Dems any more!
C at 12:33 am

Disaster for Brown! What a slap in the face from the good folk of Fife.
D at 12:33 am

The result was a victory for the Liberal Democrats with 12,391 votes to Labour's 10,591. So, in spite of what some punters were believing only a couple of minutes beforehand, the Liberal Democrats won easily. That late spurt to Labour seen in the betting was totally wrong.

Case study – using betting to influence an outcome?

Journalists covering political stories increasingly like to quote betting prices to add some zing to what they are writing. When you have little polling evidence to assess how an election is going then saying that "X is the bookies' favourite" is an easy way of describing a race.

This means that for those working to achieve a political outcome, advantage might be gained by seeking to manipulate the betting markets, by showing that your side is doing better than other indicators would suggest. There were widespread suggestions that this happened in the run-up to the 2004 White House race, when there were surges of betting support for John Kerry over and above normal market fluctuations.

The process of influencing markets in this way has been made easier by modern internet-based betting systems, where it is possible to bet for and against specific outcomes. So, if you can move the market a bit and the market then follows your money, then the cost of the exercise will be limited. For what you are doing is pump-priming the market so it moves in a particular direction and you let other punters follow. It is only when confidence starts to wane that you need to intervene again.

Extraordinarily, this case study happened only an an hour or so before the Dunfermline result. This was a classic case of what many observers regarded as market manipulation, just as the race to find a new leader of the UK Liberal Democrat party was reaching a height.

The main candidate, Sir Menzies Campbell, was considered by many to be too old at the age of 64. Another candidate had had to pull out because of newspaper allegations about his private life. And a third, who stayed in the race, also had to cope with intrusive tabloid coverage about his sexual preferences. This left just one serious challenger to Campbell – Christopher Huhne, a former journalist and member of the European Parliament, who had been in the House of Commons for less than a year.

In the first week of February there had been reports that he was doing remarkably well in private polling and the money began piling on him in the betting markets. Within a short time, much to the surprise of many insiders, he became the firm favourite, with a price where a bet of £100 would only produce a return of £80.

On February 9th 2006 ,BBC's "Question Time" programme staged a debate between the candidates.

How would they do when facing each other in front of a national TV audience?

Betting markets during the transmission of Question Time, 9 February, 2006

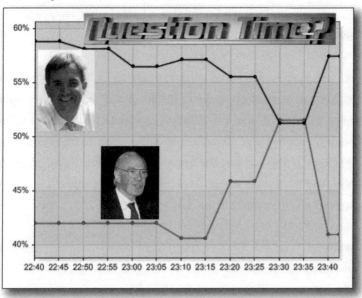

The chart above shows how the betting moved during the programme (which began at 10.30pm). Clearly those with a financial interest in the election were watching the TV debate with their laptops on their knees logged on to their betting accounts.

The general view was that Huhne did not perform very well. While the debate was progressing his price (expressed in the chart as an implied probability) began to decline and Campbell's moved up. By the end of the programme Huhne and Campbell were level-pegging on price which was a considerable change on an hour earlier. Campbell had proved himself the better, and the money went on him.

This may all be coincidental, of course, but as the chart shows there appeared to a determined effort, in the hour after the programme, to bet on Huhne and against Campbell. Certainly Huhne remained in the favourite slot.

For punters who recognised what was happening, this 'manipulation' represented a great opportunity to bet on Campbell at very good prices. He should from the objective evidence have been a strong favourite, yet this was not reflected in the price. Many people took advantage of the fact that the price was apparently being artificially controlled by somebody who was prepared to support the Huhne candidacy by 'funding' it in this way.

In the end, of course, Chris Huhne did not win so if this indeed was an attempt to use the betting markets to impact on the outcome it failed. I am certain that Huhne himself was not involved and the unusual betting was being carried out by enthusiastic supporters with deep pockets.

The main lesson from this was to trust your own judgement and be aware, all the time, that betting markets can be used by those whose interest is beyond just turning a profit.

Case study – when the betting screens were ahead of the mainstream media, the Tory leadership contest 2003

During October 2003 the then Conservative leader, Iain Duncan Smith, was coming under considerable pressure from those within his party who were not happy with his leadership. The view was that he should have been performing much better against Tony Blair, who was then starting to face the backlash on Iraq-related issues including the Hutton Inquiry.

A lively betting market developed on who would lead the Conservative party at the following general election. The big questions were whether IDS, as he was widely known, would survive and, if not, who would replace him?

He had been elected two years earlier in a ballot of the party's members after coming second in a ballot of MPs to decide the short-list of two.

By the last week of October 2003 the private briefings amongst Tory MPs about the leader had reached fever pitch and he was coming under pressure.

Even so, Duncan Smith remained the firm betting favourite to lead his party into the following election, with punters taking the view that there was apparently little stomach within the party for a potentially divisive leadership election.

On 26 October, Iain Duncan Smith appeared on television to dare his opponents to show their hand within three days or withdraw their challenges. Under the rules 25 Tory MPs needed to ask for a ballot in writing in order for there to be a confidence vote.

Within two days enough Conservative backbenchers had come forward and a ballot was set for the following day. The voting took place in a committee room at the House of Commons and the vote was timed to end at 6.30pm, with the count and a planned announcement set to take place a few minutes later.

Betting on whether IDS would survive the vote and who would lead the party at the ensuing general election was heavy and prices on the betting exchanges were fluctuating widely. As the afternoon progressed IDS's price began moving out from about 2/1 to 5/1, and then to 10/1. The vote was clearly going against him.

But then, at about 5.30pm, with an hour to go before the confidence vote ballot was due to close, there was a huge amount of activity on the two front-runners in the race, the Shadow Home Secretary, David Davis, and the Shadow Chancellor, Michael Howard. Both had been hovering in the region of 2/1 when suddenly all the money began going on Howard and punters were getting out of their David Davis positions.

There was no indication on any of the TV news channels or the radio about what was happening, but those looking at their Betfair betting screen during those few minutes could see that a distinct move had taken place – and it was not hard to work out what.

Just over an hour later the vote of confidence result was announced with Duncan Smith losing by 90 votes to 75. At 8pm David Davis made a statement that he was pulling out of the race if that meant that Michael Howard could have a clear run.

A deal had obviously been struck between Howard and Davis – an explanation of the betting moves a few hours earlier was that one or a number of the people very close to either of the camps had decided to make money on their knowledge. Those punters who were watching the markets and had correctly worked out what was happening were also able to profit.

What was very clear was the scale of the betting for Howard and against Davis. It was very apparent that this was not just a minor market correction; clearly punters were trying to get out of previous Davis positions at whatever the price. Those who followed the market and backed Howard ended up as winners.

The only downside was that the market was on who would be leader at the following general election. Punters had to wait nearly a year and a half, until election day, to collect their winnings!

Do Tories distort the betting because they have more money?

One of the questions people constantly ask about political betting is whether the betting markets are in any way predictive. After all, it is argued, the market price reflects the combined judgements of many people who have been prepared to back their opinions with cash. Surely their views should be taken more seriously than just people who have opinions but not the conviction to back them?

One of the distorting factors, it has been said, is that in the UK there is a Conservative bias amongst those who bet. There is a stereotype of young men in the City spending some of their fat bonuses on bets on the Tories. If this is the case, then betting against the Conservatives could be the smart thing to do.

It was argued that there was evidence of this at the 1997 and the 2001 general elections in the spread betting markets where punters trade on how many seats they think parties are going to get. In both elections the markets were predicting the Tories would do better in terms of seats than they actually achieved.

A more likely explanation is that at those two elections Labour performed much better in terms of seats won than the national swing suggested and the betting was following what the seat prediction calculations were throwing up.

This was monitored very closely in the weeks leading up to the 2005 general election, when the website Politicalbetting.com produced daily *balance of money* predictions which attempted to forecast the outcome based on where punters were putting their money. On the morning of the general election before the polling booths opened these were showing a projected Labour majority of 94 seats, with the Conservatives getting 186 seats, Labour 370 and the Liberal Democrats 66. As it turned out, Labour won a majority of 66 seats, with it and the

Liberal Democrats getting fewer than the betting prediction and the Conservatives more.

In this case the final seat spreads were fairly in line with the uniform national seat predictions and on that occasion the Tories did better.

Profit opportunities from combination bets

Arbitrage

Making a combination of bets so that if one bet loses another wins.

Occasionally punters who are following the markets closely will see that it is possible to make a profit by combining two or more bets which cover all eventualities. This is known as an *arbitrage* opportunity (or just an *arb*). These do not happen often and you have to move very quickly to benefit as the case study below shows.

An arb case study – the Sunday that Gordon Brown became favourite to lead Labour at the 2005 general election

On the weekend of May 15/16 2004, a rumour swept through the Westminster village about a family problem for Tony and Cherie Blair that people concluded would possibly lead to him wanting to step down as Prime Minister within a matter of weeks. The media showed great restraint, and the rumour was never reported.

But punters in the know saw an opportunity for profit and by 10.12am on the Sunday morning heavy betting on Gordon Brown on Betfair made him favourite to be Labour leader at the following general election. This was the first time he'd been ahead of Tony Blair, whose price eased to below evens. At the same time it was possible to bet with William Hill that Blair would not be leader at a price of 2/1.

Two bookmakers were offering odds on Blair going before the General Election that were so out of line with the Betfair Labour leader price that it was possible to bet against Blair in one market and bet on him in another and be sure of a certain profit.

At one point you could back Blair on Betfair at evens and bet against him on William Hill at 2/1.

The arbitrage opportunity came because these two bets were opposites and their average price was greater than evens.

	Betfair	William Hill
The market	Who will be Labour leader at the next general election	Tony Blair will not be leader at the next general election
Price at 10.12am Sunday May 16th 2004	Evens	2/1
Bet possibility	A £50 winning bet would produce a profit of £50. A losing bet a loss of £50	A £33 winning bet would produce a profit of £66. A losing bet a loss of £33
Possible outcomes	If Blair **remained** you win (£50 less cost of William Bet) = £17 If Blair **did not remain** you win (£66 less cost of Betfair bet) = £16	

So a punter who managed to place both bets on that Sunday was in for a certain profit whether or not Blair remained. The only down-side was that you had to tie money up, in this case £83, for perhaps, a year.

Arb betting tactics

The opportunities do not come up very often but when they do you have to act very fast because there is one thing that is for sure – if you have seen it then others will have noticed it as well.

You need to think through very carefully whether your interpretation of the rules of each market is correct. Could you be misleading yourself?

You then have to make an instant judgement about which bet is going to be most difficult to get on – in this case it was the one from William Hill.

As it turned out, on that Sunday the William Hill price did not last long and was tightened. On Betfair the Blair price began to move as well so that by 11am the opportunity did not exist.

Whatever, there is something very satisfying about placing successful arbs. You really do feel you are beating the system.

Other combining bet possibilities

The example above was a true arb because you win in all circumstances. Quite often *near arbs* are possible which, while not giving you a guaranteed profit, can be very attractive.

Three and a half months before the May 2005 general election, one of the regular contributors to Politicalbetting.com, who files under the name of Jon, came forward with this ingenious plan.

> *His idea was was simple. Buy the Tories at £10 a seat, at the then price of 195 on the spread-betting markets. At the same time back Labour for £1000 to win most seats at the general election at the prevailing price of 0.18/1 on Betfair. At that*

price you win £180 if Labour does get most seats but lose
£1000 if it doesn't.

His reasoning was that if the Tories fell short of the 195 target then you are still a net winner with your Labour bet until Michael Howard's party drops to below 177 seats. For you to lose your 'Labour to win most seats' bet then the Tories would have had to win something like 280 seats and your losses will be mostly offset by your spread betting winnings. Once the Tories are over 295 seats you would back in a profit situation.

The bet profile is shown in the table below.

Tory seat result	Profit/loss
177 or less	lose £10 for each seat.
177-195	end up as an overall winner, with the profits from the Labour bet (£180) more than covering the losses on the spread bet
196-280 (approx) seats	win on both bets
281-295 seats	lose up to a maximum of £150
295+	spread betting profit exceeds your Labour most seats losses

As it turned out the Tories ended up with 198 seats so both the spread bet and the Labour win bet would have ended up as winners.

I liked the thinking behind this and will be looking out for other possibilities in future general elections.

Betting Tactics
Following the Polls

6
Betting Tactics Following the Polls

What are polls?

An opinion poll is a means for determining how people think about an issue by asking a small number for their views and then extrapolating their responses to the group as a whole. They were used for the first time, in the form we know them today, ahead of the 1936 White House race between the Republican, Alf Landon and the Democrat, Franklin D. Roosevelt.

By polling a demographically representative sample the pioneer of the business, George Gallup, correctly predicted Roosevelt's landslide. This contrasted starkly with a survey that the magazine Literary Digest carried out by mailing millions of post-cards asking people which way they were going to vote. A total of 2.3 million of them were returned, and they indicated that Landon was in the lead. The issue, it transpired, was that readers of the magazine tended to be more affluent and their allegiances were closer to the Republicans. Nothing was done to correct the bias, so even with its massive sample this poll got the prediction wrong.

In the UK the Gallup organisation had its first big success with the 1945 general election. Received opinion had it that a grateful nation would return the wartime leader, Winston Churchill and his Conservative Party. The Gallup surveys suggested a Labour victory, which turned out to be correct.

Since then opinion polls have become a very familiar part of the political scene, with at least five major national surveys taking place every month.

The main UK political pollsters

The main polling organisations in the UK are-

1. British Polling Index
2. Communicate Research
3. ICM
4. Ipsos Mori
5. NOP
6. Populus
7. YouGov

Some of the main characteristics of these companies are explained in the table opposite.

Pollster	Main Media Client	Methodology	2005 Election performance	Timing
British Polling Index (The firm contracts out the fieldwork process to another pollster.)	Occasional surveys for the *Mail on Sunday* since 2005.	Internet panel similar to YouGov developed by the University of Essex.	Con 33 (0) Lab 37 (+1) LD 21 (-2) In second place overall.	BPIX surveys are commissioned by the *Mail on Sunday* on an intermittent basis and there is no pattern.
Communicate Research (The firm contracts out the fieldwork process and often uses the ICM off-shoot, ICM-Direct.)	Monthly surveys for the *Independent* since October 2006.	Telephone interviews using standard demographic weightings, but does not use past vote weighting to seek to ensure politically balanced samples.	Con 31 (-2) Lab 39 (+3) LD 23 (0) Came last of all the pollsters, although its final survey took place well before all the others.	The firm tends to carry out its main surveys on the third weekend of each month, with the results being published on the following Wednesday or Thursday.
ICM (The firm carries out its own fieldwork and carries out such work for several other telephone pollsters.)	Monthly surveys for the *Guardian* since 1984.	Telephone interviews with what is known as "past vote weighting" to ensure a politically balanced sample on top of standard demographic weightings.	Con 32 (-1) Lab 38 (+2) LD 22 (-1) A solid performance keeping up with its good record at UK general elections.	The fieldwork for ICM surveys generally takes place over the third weekend each month with the results being published on the following Tuesday or Wednesday.
Ipsos Mori (The firm carries out all its own fieldwork.)	Monthly surveys for a range of clients.	Face-to-face interviews based on quota sampling. Headline figures are restricted to those saying they are "100% certain to vote". Occasionally carries out telephone surveys.	Con 33 (0) Lab 38 (+2) LD 23 (0) A good performance only marred by the slight overstatement of Labour.	The firm's main political surveys tend to take place during the first half of the month and can be published at any time thereafter depending on which newspapers decide to carry it.
NOP	Regular survey for the Independent until 2005 general election.	Telephone interviews with what is known as "past vote weighting" to ensure a politically balanced sample.	Con 33 (0) Lab 36 (0) LD 23 (0) A great performance coming top with all the main numbers right.	In spite of being the most accurate pollster at the 2005 general election, the firm did not have a regular media client in early 2007.
Populus (The firm contracts out the telephone fieldwork process and for the majority of its surveys for *The Times* it uses ICM-Direct.)	Monthly surveys for *The Times* since 2002.	Telephone interviews with what is known as "past vote weighting" to ensure a politically balanced sample.	Con 32 (-1) Lab 38 (+2) LD 21 (-2) A solid performance in its first General Election.	*The Times* surveys almost always takes place during the first weekend of the month and the results are invariably published on the following Tuesday.
YouGov (It handles all its own online field-work and also operates on a "white label" basis carrying out online-based surveys for other firms.)	Monthly surveys for the *Daily Telegraph* since 2003.	Internet based approach amongst members of its polling panel on whom it maintains a mass of back data to ensure politically balanced samples.	Con 32 (-1) Lab 37 (+1) LD 24 (+1) A good performance.	The main survey for the *Daily Telegraph* usually takes places during the final week of the month with the results being published on the Friday.

Note. "Past vote weighting" is a procedure used by all but one of the telephone pollsters to ensure that their samples are politically representative. Respondents are asked how they voted at the previous General Election and the responses were weighted in line with the actual result with an allowance being made for a level of misremembering. Thus we know that 36% of people voted Labour in May 2005 and if 50% of those in a survey say that this was what they did then an adjustment is made to cover part, but not all, of the discrepancy.

The '2005 election performance' column shows the result of the final poll that the firm carried out with, in the brackets, how far this was out with each party compared with the actual result.

Opinion polls and Betting

A large part of political betting is about forecasting the results of elections, and probably the most important tool that we have are the polls. As well as telling us how people say they would vote, the polls show how different political leaders are being perceived and what issues are on voters' minds. They also play a critical part in party leadership elections, when those party members and others with votes can see how each of the different candidates is going down with the public.

Opinion polls can be important in determining whether someone stays in their job – they can make or break political careers. They also help the parties hone their message so that what they say and how they say it is best received by the voters.

In the betting markets it is usually the opinion polls that help determine how punters are viewing things; there is little doubt that the polls drive the odds up and down. Usually, when there is a significant change in prices, it is as a result of a poll.

How the polls are reported

Quite often it is not the polls themselves that matter, but how they are reported and what aspect the commissioning media organisation wishes to put the focus on. Sometimes, if the main voting intention outcome is not something that the newspaper wants to highlight, then another aspect of the poll will be featured.

The surveys that get the most attention and are likely to have an impact on betting markets are the monthly polls by ICM, Populus and YouGov in the *Guardian*, *The Times* and the *Daily Telegraph*. All these papers take their own polls very seriously and tend to splash their findings if they are particularly newsworthy. Sometimes, what is clearly a 'dud' conclusion is given wide prominence and can affect the betting.

Case Studies

Tory leadership contest 2005 – a bonanza for punters who believed the polls

In terms of its popularity with punters the Tory leadership election of 2005 was a major event. Punters like betting on personalities they know and there was a big betting interest right through from May to December 2005.

Contests like this are great for the pollsters and a wide range of different options can be backed. Not only was the general public being asked repeatedly who they preferred, but there were constant comparisons of who would be best to take on Labour.

There were many polls. The UK Polling Report web site lists 16 polls, which were in addition to the seven separate polls of Tory party membership – the body that ultimately decides the leadership. It was this latter group of surveys that dominated the thinking of smart punters, as it was the party membership – and not the public at large – that made the final decision. Four years earlier in July 2001 the internet pollster, YouGov, pulled off an amazing coup when it found that party members were splitting 61%-39% in favour of Iain Duncan Smith over Ken Clarke – the two Tory MPs who had been selected by the parliamentary party to have their names put to the membership. This poll had been correct to within one percent.

Such extraordinary level of accuracy gave those who were aware of YouGov's record a lot of confidence. In the immediate aftermath of David Cameron's famous Blackpool conference speech in October 2005, a YouGov party members' poll had him getting the support of 66%. This increased to 77% a fortnight later, but by early November Cameron was back at the 67%-68% level in the run-off against the then Shadow Home Secretary, David Davis. The final members' poll, published three days before the count, had Cameron on 67%. The actual result was, like in 2001, within one per cent of the pollster's forecast – a major achievement and gamblers who had followed the firm made a lot of money.

The one polling blip during the campaign provided confident gamblers with a great opportunity to get on the Cameron bandwagon, at what turned out to be bargain prices. On November 9th 2005 *The Times* carried the result of its monthly Populus survey where those declaring that they were Conservative supporters, as opposed to members, said they rated Davis to Cameron as "best leader" by 50% to 37%. This was splashed by the paper and led to big moves against Cameron on the betting markets.

Before this poll came out, the Betfair price on Cameron had been as tight as 0.07/1. In the immediate aftermath of the report it moved out to 0.4/1, before tightening again. So a £100 Cameron bet the night before would have produced a profit of just £7. By noon the following day the same bet would have produced a profit of £40. These are colossal differences and vividly illustrate the power of polls – or, more precisely, the reporting of polls – to have a big impact on political betting.

Betting on David Davis in the Tory leadership contest 2005

The chart for November 9 to 11th 2005 shows the implied probability of David Davis winning (based on the prevailing best betting prices) following the report in *The Times* of the poll. Two days later, when Davis faced a severe grilling by Jeremy Paxman on BBC's Newsnight programme, the market was on its way back to "normal".

The paper did not give as much prominence to other findings showing that Cameron was judged more likely to win an election and unite the party than Davis. So, the lesson is: it is often the reporting of polls, and not the fine detail, that gambling markets react to.

Liberal Democrat leadership race 2006 – the shadowy world of private and voodoo polls

Would YouGov get it right with the Liberal Democrats as well?

YouGov's extraordinary achievement in getting the Tory leadership ballot correct to within one per cent for the second time in four years had a big impact on the Liberal Democrat leadership race that started only a month afterwards. Although the parties are very different, many punters made the assumption that if YouGov polling of the Tory membership was so accurate then it was a fair bet to assume that it would perform reasonably well with the Liberal Democrats as well.

Even before the former leader, Charles Kennedy, had announced his resignation, YouGov carried out a membership poll for the *Daily Telegraph* showing that Sir Menzies Campbell had a 49% level of support, against 21% for Simon Hughes – the person many believed had the backing of the party activists. The margin between the front-runners looked too big a gap for Hughes to overhaul; however, he stayed in the race in spite of revelations in the tabloids about his personal life.

The real surprise was the emergence of Chris Huhne – a former Euro MP, who had only been elected to the Westminster parliament nine months before. He, along with Hughes and Campbell, became the three names that were put before the membership in a postal ballot.

Money started going on Huhne and within a short time he became the betting favourite, which surprised a lot of people. But there was a belief that an effort was being made to promote his position by one or more individuals who were putting enough money on him on the betting exchanges so that he appeared favourite. If this *was* happening, it was a good strategy because he was almost unknown at the start of the contest.

How punters were confused by privately commissioned surveys

What was needed was another YouGov members' poll, but no media backer seemed to want to fund one. So as all the money, apparently, was going on Huhne, nobody quite knew what was really happening. Then came word that YouGov was carrying out membership surveys for first one, and then two, private clients.

Unlike normal opinion polls that appear in the newspapers there is no requirement under the transparency rules to which most of the leading pollsters subscribe to publish private polling data.

Given YouGov successes with the Tory contest, almost everybody associated with the contest was keen to see what these had produced.

Rumours started to develop that the first poll, said to have been commissioned by a wealthy Campbell backer, was showing the 64 year-old ahead, but by nothing like the margin that his supporters must have hoped for. The unknown Huhne was said to be in a respectable second place and this was why, it was suggested, that the full details were not being released.

Then another private poll was commissioned, this time by a Huhne backer, who immediately authorised that the results be published, as they showed that his man was ahead by 4%. When the full details of this survey were made available people started to question the way it had been carried out. For, unlike normal polling surveys, the question of which of the candidates the respondents would vote for was asked at the end and not the start.

It is standard practice with almost all polling to ask the voting intention question right at the start to ensure that the process of testing opinion is not in fact influencing the outcome.

The survey asked people if they thought "Sir Menzies Campbell was too old to be leader of the Liberal Democrats". It then asked which candidate would most appeal to women, and to "attract young people to vote for the Liberal Democrats". Another question asked if people thought that "Simon Hughes was unreliable".

All of this, it was argued, had highlighted the negatives about Campbell, so that by the time they got round to answering the voting intention question they were less positive about him.

That was fine, until details of the earlier private poll, showing Campbell ahead, were made public and precisely the same approach had been taken. The pre-voting intention questions had put the emphasis on Campbell's positive attributes over his younger rival.

So two polls from the same polling organisation carried out within days of each other were suggesting very different outcomes. What should political gamblers do?

The **Independent** and the **Guardian** surveys

The waters got even murkier with another bizarre twist five days before postal ballots had to be in. Both the *Guardian* and the *Independent* newspapers carried out surveys of attendees at the same hustings meeting in London where the three contenders faced questioning from several hundred party members and others. The problem for gamblers and others trying to forecast the election was that the two papers came out with completely different findings. It was as though they had been at different meetings.

The *Guardian* reported that it had spoken to 422 people who were there and found Huhne had 152 first preferences (36%), Ming 124 (29%) and Hughes 87 (21%).

But the *Independent's* survey talking to 100 people at the same meeting overwhelmingly pointed to a victory for Ming Campbell. The acting leader had 51 giving him their first preference with 31 to Simon Hughes and just 18 to Chris Huhne.

Neither of these could be described as proper opinion polls, because nobody knew whether those who attended a meeting in Central London on a cold February evening were an accurate sample. In spite of this, both surveys were presented by the papers as tests of opinion within the party and they devoted a lot of space to them.

As a risk-averse gambler, I could not choose between the two front-runners. I arranged it so that my financial position was the same whether Campbell or Huhne was declared the winner.

The Liberal Democrat leadership election has been recounted at length here because it was a huge betting event, and there are important lessons to be learned about what – and what not to – take into account. Be very sceptical about newspaper-type surveys which are not proper polls following normal rules, and be wary about privately commissioned polls. The latter have been produced for a reason – usually to promote a candidate or a point of view and not to help political punters or election forecasters.

November 2nd, 2004 – the night John Kerry thought he would wake up as President

Exit polls for the US presidential election 2004

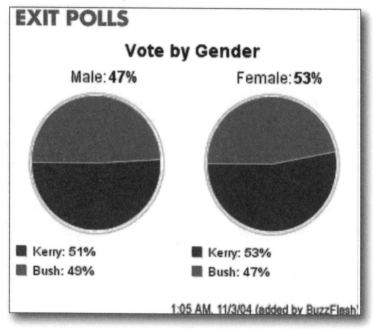

At 1.05am EST on November 3rd 2004 the US news channel, CNN, showed the above graphic on the screen illustrating the result of an exit poll in Ohio – the key state that Senator John Kerry had to win if he was to beat George W. Bush for the Presidency.

The message was clear. Kerry was ahead in Ohio, and the chances were that the State would give him enough votes in the electoral college to become the next President. The exit polls, and the leaks about them the previous evening, had completely turned the White House race betting market on its head.

When the polling stations had opened the day before, Bush was an odds on favourite to win. By the time the exit polls had been published, things had changed dramatically.

Those few hours saw the biggest political gambling spree ever seen with tens of millions of pounds being wagered in the UK alone.

The exit poll results had been produced for a consortium of the major US news organisations, working as the National Election Pool (NEP). They were based on interviews with voters in 49 States. In the days and months that followed there were huge investigations into why the NEP figures, particularly in key states such as Ohio, had been wrong.

The co-director of NEP, Warren Mitofsky, was quoted as saying,

> *the Kerry voters were more anxious to participate in our exit polls than the Bush voters*

Another suggestion was that women were marginally more pro-Kerry, and in the early polls they represented 58% of the sampled voters.

Whatever the post-election explanations, this was completely irrelevant to the betting. Punters were making decisions in an instant, and the conclusion from what was being reported about the polls was that Kerry had won. Many gamblers lost a lot of money that night. One of the bosses of a spread betting company told me later that it was one of their most profitable sessions ever.

1992 UK general election – when a 1% Tory poll deficit became an 8% lead in real votes

Nearly fifteen years after the 1992 UK general election, Nick Sparrow, the head of the pioneering pollster ICM, was still describing what happened to his industry on April 10th of that year as a "debacle". Quite simply, the pollsters got it wrong and gamblers, who had wagered money based on what they were reporting, lost out substantially.

The final opinion polls gave the Conservatives between 38% and 39% of the vote, about 1% behind Labour. On the day itself, exit polls were carried out and everything was pointing to a hung parliament. But when the votes were counted, the Conservatives, under the leadership of John Major, had a margin of 7.6% over Labour – something that was not anticipated at all in the dozens of surveys that had been carried out in the previous weeks. As a result of this failure to predict the result, the Market Research Society held an inquiry into the reasons why the polls had been so much at variance with actual public opinion.

In the months and years that followed, several of the polling organisations put in measures to deal with what appeared to be a systemic problem – the tendency of polls, when tested against real results, to over-estimate the proportion of Labour voters and to underestimate the Conservative share.

By 2007 none of the polling organisations which had carried out those 1992 polls were still around carrying out surveys in the same way. Some had left the UK market, while others had adapted their methodologies to deal with the challenges.

The new ways of dealing with the pro-Labour polling bias

Past vote weighting

One of the biggest changes that was introduced was past vote weighting – the process in which pollsters like ICM and, now, Populus seek to ensure they have balanced samples by weighting their results in line with what respondents said they did last time (taking into account a level of misremembering).

A challenge is that, for reasons that I have never seen satisfactorily explained, the process of telephone polling almost always seems to produce many more people saying they voted Labour at the previous general election than actually did so. Thus, in all the published data in the year after the 2005 general election from the two polling firms that ask how respondents voted last time, an average of more than 44% said Labour.

Given that we know from the actual result that the Labour vote share was 36.2% then something is not right with the samples. Maybe there is something about those who voted Labour that makes them more likely than voters for other parties to respond to unsolicited randomised phone calls from the pollsters? Who knows? But ICM and Populus adjust their figures to take this into account.

Misremembering

They do not adjust fully, because it is accepted that there is a level of misremembering. A number of people forget how they voted the time before, or they give wrong information. There is a tendency to say you voted for the winner of the last general election even if you did not. To deal with this the pollsters have their own formulas which average out what has been said to them in a run of surveys. The result at the end of 2006 with ICM was that if 44% of those questioned in a survey said they had voted Labour then their responses were scaled down to 39%, which was still a bigger proportion than actually had voted for the party in May 2005. Populus at that time was scaling down to about 40%.

Turnouts

Another factor that it was thought was causing the overstatement of Labour was differential turnout, with its party supporters being less inclined to actually vote than those of other parties. To deal with this, almost all the non-internet pollsters ask how likely it is that people will vote, usually asking them to rate it on a scale from 0-10.

The Ipsos-Mori firm has a very harsh way of dealing with the turnout figures. In its headline party shares it only uses those who say they are "100% certain to vote". The pollster publishes on its website both sets of figures and there is usually a big cut-back in the Labour proportion when you only include those absolutely certain to vote.

Another issue is that always in every survey quite a high proportion say they will vote, but refuse, or say they do not know when asked, which party it will be for. If a party is unpopular you get the phenomenon of the "shy Tories" – or later, the "shy Blairites". To deal with this, Populus and ICM make a calculation, sometimes called the "spiral of silence adjustment", which takes into account part of what people said they did at the previous general election.

Another pollster, Communicate Research, seeks to force an answer out of respondents by asking those who refuse, or say they do not know, how they would vote "if voting was a legal requirement".

There is one possible sting in the tail here. For although the firms make these calculations in surveys where a voting intention question is asked, they do not do so with their other polls.

The firms carry out regular 'omnibus' surveys for a range of clients, who each pay to have their questions put to the public. Often political questions are asked, but the responses are not adjusted in the same way that they would be in a voting intention survey.

Polling data from surveys, where there is no adjusting factor to deal with politically unrepresentative samples, should be treated with care. The chances are that they will include the opinions of a much higher proportion of 2005 Labour voters as compared with what actually happened.

The internet pollster, YouGov, carries out its polls amongst members of its polling panel on who it retains an enormous amount of data, including what they said they did at the last general election. It is thus in a position to make calculations similar to what ICM and Populus do.

Polling outcomes that you should be careful about

Political punters are very much reliant on how newspapers and the rest of the media *report* polls, rather than the actual surveys themselves. Sometimes what are presented as proper voting intention polls are not in fact that, and there is a danger that punters can be misled. The most common pitfalls are the following.

Individual constituency surveys

Every pollster that I have ever discussed this with has told me how difficult it is polling an individual constituency, either ahead of a by-election or a general election. The challenge is in getting a representative sample in a relatively small area compared with the nation or region as a whole. Thus in June 2006 a poll ahead of the Blaenau Gwent parliamentary by-election reported that Labour were beating off the Independent by 47%-35% and would recover the seat lost a year beforehand. This led to Labour becoming the odds on favourite. On polling day the Independent beat off the Labour challenge by 47%-37%.

Be very sceptical of such polls!

Forced choice questions

Such as:

> "If you had to choose, which would you prefer to see after the
> next election, a Conservative government led by David Cameron
> or a Labour government led by Gordon Brown?"

There is no option to state a party other than the Conservatives and Labour, and it is highly likely that the pollster's turnout filters have not been used. The results are very interesting and might give an indication of possible tactical voting, but the results are not, as sometimes suggested, possible vote shares in a general election.

Treat with care!

Named leaders questions

Such as:

> "How would you vote if Brown was leading Labour, Cameron the
> Conservatives and Campbell the Lib Dems?"

These are very common during party leadership races and quite often they are linked to the main voting share outcomes in the same poll. Normally pollsters, like Populus and ICM, will apply the same filters as with their standard voting intention questions – but not always. The results are, of course, more hypothetical than the standard questions.

Treat with some caution!

Personal ratings questions
Such as:

> *"How do you think David Cameron is doing in his job as leader of the Conservatives?"*

Normally the filters on turnout that are used with voting intention questions are not applied here, so you might be seeing the views of a large number of non-voters – a group which has little relevance to election gamblers.

Don't overstate their importance.

The Process of Betting
The Key Decisions
That Have To Be Taken

7
The Process of Betting
The Key Decisions
That Have to be Taken

Making your selection

This chapter looks at some of the processes that a successful political punter ought to go through before making a bet. Anybody can splash out money based on instinct, but the successful gamblers will have examined the possibilities in more detail and have sought to take an objective view.

Doing your research

The great luxury that political punters usually have is time. Decisions do not usually need to be made in an instant, and time can be taken to look into the background of your proposed punt.

Everything has been made so much easier with the internet. A vast array of data is available within seconds. For example, if you want to find out how George Bush was polling at a precise stage before the 2004 White House race, this information is on the web, available 24/7.

In the appendix there is a list of good sites that I refer to regularly to get a sense of what is going on. And on many occasions what I have found has stopped me making a bet, or opened up a possibility that I did not think existed.

The only downside, of course, is that all the information is available to everybody else. You have got to use it smarter.

Betting odds search engines

Comparing prices on the next general election

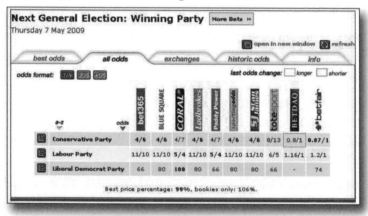

Perhaps the most obvious betting tools that the internet has provided are the betting odds search engines, such as Bestbetting or OddsChecker. These compile in real time the latest odds that are available from thousands of different markets from dozen of different bookmakers so that you are able to find out in a fraction of a second where the best place is for you to put your bet on.

I should declare an interest. The idea of what was to become Bestbetting.com was jointly created by me and my son, Robert, on Christmas day 1999 in the days of using the internet with slow telephone modems. I was trying to find out different prices on the first London Mayoral race in 2000.

Surely there was a better way than labouriously going to each online bookmaker's site to find out if they had a market and then to check the prices?

Robert took the idea up and this has developed into a major business with a big turnover. Sadly he has a much bigger stake in the company than me!

What happens with Bestbetting and similar sites is that you find your chosen market and up pops either a table showing the best prices that are available for each of the runners, or a fuller chart with the range of bookmaker options. It can be quite extraordinary to see how much variation there is and clearly you want the best price.

The search engines normally show betting exchange prices as well as those from the standard bookmakers and in some cases they show spread betting prices as well. Bestbetting also has a useful historical odds facility so you can see how a market has developed and which way it is going.

The odds are constantly updated day and night and the sites have made the process of betting that much easier. These firms make their money from commissions paid to them by the online bookmakers.

Political betting – how objective is your judgement?

What is very clear is that there are two very distinct groups of people who like to bet on politics–

- those with a passionate interest who follow things very closely, and

- those who like betting, but only come to political markets when a big event is coming up.

Most of those in the former group have very strong allegiances, and are often in danger of seeing things through rose-coloured spectacles. In many instances they will only bet on a party or person that they want to win. Sometimes the process of making a bet is a way of them proving their support and loyalty.

In other instances this works the other way round. The driving force behind someone's betting is that a person or a party should not succeed. The danger is that their very passion and strong beliefs will cause them to read things wrongly.

Another element that can distort someone's judgment is having made a bet already. You have gone through the process of weighing up the options, you make your choice, and you put your money on. You can then be in danger of only reading and taking notice of developments supporting your initial judgment.

The good political gambler who is doing it for profit has to be aware of all these factors, has to view all the information available with great rigour, and has to be prepared to change his or her mind when things change.

Is your planned bet good value?

A bet becomes good value only if the *chances of your bet coming good is better than the betting odds suggest*. Because political punters usually have more time to make an evaluation it is recommend that you follow a fairly rigorous process to assess this.

Make your own book
A number of experienced gamblers make a theoretical book. They study the form, evaluate all the information that they know, and without looking at the prices on offer, write down their own prediction of what the betting should be. They express the odds in percentages and make sure they add up to 100 (or close to it). They then compare their estimates with the actual odds on offer. If there are any major differences with no obvious explanation, they might have discovered some value.

If, like many political gamblers these days, you are using a betting exchange, ask yourself at what price you would be prepared to back and at what point you would prefer to lay. After all, if one price is too short, it follows that another, somewhere, must be too long and therefore represents value.

Watch out for the Hype

The Hype will often alert you to the existence of value. As seasoned gamblers say repeatedly, markets do not react, they overreact. When they do so, there is almost certain to be value created somewhere. To exploit it, you will be moving against the crowd. After all, there cannot be much value in following the crowd because, by definition, the crowd will have driven the value out. If you think the crowd is right, let it pass. If the crowd is wrong, you have identified value.

Be decisive

Be decisive when you see good value. Top prices don't last long, and if you miss them, don't chase the price down. Resist the temptation to be greedy and wait for a bigger one. The professional gambler would say here that if the price does drift then bet again. This requires a lot of confidence in your first assessment but, after all, if it was value at the lower price, it is even better value now.

Be ready to back more than one candidate, party or other runner in a race. Some people think this is wrong because you are betting against yourself. I think it is wrong to imagine only one of the prices per event is sufficiently wrong to represent value. Thus, as I write this at the start of 2007, I have two runners in the US Democratic party nomination race – one has moved in sharply the other has moved out. Both seemed good value when I placed the bets.

The greater the value the bigger the bet

A good rule is: the greater the value the bigger the bet. It can be hard to get your head around this one because most of us are conditioned to putting small amounts on outsiders and bigger amounts on favourites.

In fact we should be graduating our bets according to the value in them. One of my best recent bets was getting 200/1 and 150/1 on Chris Huhne in the Liberal Democrat leadership race, after it looked certain that he was going to get enough fellow MPs to nominate him. I put as much on as I could at those prices. Within two weeks Huhne's price had tightened to below evens and I was able to lay masses of this off and ensure that whoever won the election I was a big financial winner.

Good value bets are not always winners

The fact that you are following the rules on value does not mean that each and every position you enter into will be a winner. An assessment that an outcome is 20% likely is exactly that, and the chances are that it will lose. The critical thing is that the price you bet on is better than your probability assessment.

Sometimes you can end up with big losses – even if you have followed the above rules. In fact, it would be quite extraordinary if it was any other way.

Case Study – a value bet that was a big loser

Because of the personalities involved, and the fact that it takes place within the capital, there is always very heavy betting in the London Mayoral Election which takes place every four years. In 2004 I took a big position that Ken Livingstone was not going to do it. I was wrong but, I would argue, it was still a good value bet because the average price I got on him failing was about 8/1.

In 2000 this was won by Livingstone, who was then standing as an Independent, over the colourful former Conservative minister, Steve Norris. A characteristic of that race was that Livingstone's margin was substantially smaller than the polls had been predicting and that Norris had done a lot better. The opinion polls had given Livingstone leads over Norris ranging from 34% to 57%. It was actually 11.9%.

This was helped by the fact that there are substantially higher turnout rates in outer Tory and Liberal Democrat areas than in Labour's inner-city strongholds, giving them a disproportionate effect on the outcome.

In the previous two all-London local elections the Conservatives had won more votes than Labour – even though the party was then going through a turbulent time nationally. That looked likely to happen again.

The big unknown for the 2004 race was how Livingstone would fare as the official Labour candidate and not the independent of four years earlier.

Would Tory voters switch to support Livingstone?

Taking everything into account, my conclusion was that the Livingstone price was too tight and that there was a chance that he would be beaten. As it turned out, I was wrong. But it was a value bet.

Do you understand the precise terms of your punt?

One of the problems bookmakers repeatedly have with political bets is that they have not framed the detailed rules of the market tightly enough.

With a sporting event, like a horse race or a football match, these problems happen only rarely because it is clear for all to see that if you back, say, Manchester City to beat Manchester United and the result is 0-2, then you have lost. With politics things can be more complicated.

If problems arise then what precedents exist indicate that bookmakers will fall back on the precise terms they used when they established the market, even if this results in punters, who think they have backed a winner, not being paid.

The issue is particularly difficult for the betting exchanges because here the bookmaker stands in the middle of two sets of punters – those who have put their money on a particular eventuality happening and those who have bet against.

Case Study – settling the 2006 US Senate Midterms Market

By far the most important political event in the world in 2006 was the defeat of the Republicans in the US midterm elections in November. The party lost control of both parts of Congress – the House of Representative and the Senate – both apparently falling to a big surge in Democrat support.

"Apparently", because that was not the way it looked to Betfair – the UK company that has become the world's biggest betting exchange. The terms of their market stated:

> "Which of these parties will have more seats in the US Senate following the 2006 US Senate Elections – Republicans or Democrats?"

After the election, the Republicans had to cede control after winning only 49 of the 100 seats. The problem for the Democrats was that only 49 of their Senators had campaigned for office as members of the party. Another well-known Democrat, Joseph Lieberman, won re-election as the "Connecticut For Lieberman" party candidate – an independent political party he created after losing the 2006 Democratic primary election to Ned Lamont. He had told voters that if elected he would sit as part of the Democratic Senate caucus.

The other oddity was Bernie Sanders who won in Vermont as an Independent, but had said that he would caucus with the Democrats and is counted as a Democrat for the purposes of committee assignments. He had originally been selected as the Democratic candidate, but had changed to being an Independent. There was no Democratic candidate in the state.

An added complication for Betfair was that the British Labour MP, Nick Palmer, had written to Betfair ahead of the election asking for clarification about Lieberman's position and had received a written reply confirming that if Lieberman won he would be regarded as a Democrat. Palmer had posted this information on the Politcalbetting.com website, influencing, no doubt, a number of other punters in the process.

There was a big argument immediately after the election between those punters who had backed the Republicans to hold on and those who had taken a punt, at quite long odds in many cases, on the Democrats doing it. Eventually Betfair ruled that Sanders and Lieberman would not count as Democrats, even though for the purposes of power in the Senate they were regarded as members of the Democrat group.

So according to Betfair the result had been a 49-49 dead heat and the rules in relation to settling a market in relation to a tie came into operation

Case Study – settling the North Korean missile test market

This had echoes of a row earlier in the year involving the Dublin-based betting exchange, Tradesports. At the start of July 2006, the main international story was the launch by the North Koreans – on American Independence Day – of a long-range missile.

The possibility that such a move would happen had been the subject of a Tradesport market, established a fortnight earlier, for or against the probability that North Korea would:

"launch a test missile leaving its airspace by the end of July 2006?"

You might think that those who had bet "yes" would end up winners, while those who had bet "no" would have lost.

Wrong!

Because of the way Tradesports interpreted the rules of the market, the test did not happen and it was the "no" punters who won.

Tradesports stuck by the detailed requirements of the bet that *"the source used to confirm a test missile being launched and leaving North Korean airspace will be the U.S. Department of Defence."*

So, statements on July 4, by the White House Press Secretary, Tony Snow, and the National Security Advisor, Steve Hadley, that there had been multiple launches did not suffice.

According to the SmartMoney site, Tradesports spokesman, Matt Bonner, said they made, "numerous efforts to receive direct confirmation from the DoD" but were told

"no statement involving the missile test and North Korean airspace would be forthcoming, as those specifics are considered a matter of national intelligence/security."

What it came down to was that punters were betting on whether the US Department of Defence would produce a statement of confirmation – not whether the North Koreans would fire a missile!

In these cases the betting exchange sits between two sets of punters: those who bet one way and those who bet the other. If it had ruled the other way then the "no" backers could have argued that the strict terms of the bet they had entered into had not been met.

TradeSports made this statement,

"We apologise for any inconvenience caused. In particular we

apologise to those members who interpreted a 'contract intention'
without having assimilated the Contract rules before they traded..."

The firm promised to make some changes to the way it settles markets like this.

What is clear, from both the Betfair and Tradesports cases, is that bookmakers will generally stick by the precise literal terms of the bet if a dispute occurs. It is best to assume that this will happen even if there is evidence to the contrary, like the email to the Labour MP in the US Senate row.

Are you betting the way you think you are betting?

A very common occurrence – with even the most seasoned gamblers – is that they click the wrong button on their computer screens. Always check, and double check, that you have the correct selection at the price you think it should be, and that you are *backing* when you want to back and are *laying* when you want to lay. Once you have clicked to confirm, then you are usually lumbered. A novice might be able to persuade the betting exchange or spread betting firm to change, but you cannot be sure of it.

Are you fully aware of the risk you are taking?

With spread betting or using a betting exchange you could be taking on quite a financial risk. If you are laying a £10 bet at 20/1 then you could lose £200 if that option won. With a spread bet on, say, the number of seats a party will get at a general election, it is often easy to be misled by the stake amount. Suppose you were buying Labour at 370 seats at £20, you stand to lose your stake level multiplied by the number of seats the party falls short if that is indeed what happens. So if Labour win only 320 seats, you have lost £1,000.

Credit accounts with spread betting firms are very useful because you do not have to put any money upfront – but there are normally no stop levels.

Finally – are you sure that this is what you want to do?

- Before making that final click, just consider again what you are doing.

- Are you really certain that this is worth the risk?

- Why are you betting the way you are?

- Why are you doing it now – would delaying the bet give you a better chance to assess whether your planned option will actually happen?

- Is your bet good value?

Ten Tips for
Profitable Political Betting

8

Ten Tips for
Profitable Political Betting

1. If the person or party you want to back is a strong election favourite, the earlier you get your money on the better.

2. If you want to bet on anything other than a strong favourite, wait until after the polling booths have opened to get a better price.

3. Punters have a strong herd instinct and can often lose money following other punters who are losers.

4. On US election nights always assume that the leaks of exit polls and the exit polls themselves are over-stating the Democrats' strength.

5. In races for the Democrat or Republican nomination in the US assume that early opinion polls are little more than tests of recognition not popular support.

6. In Conservative leadership contests **always** bet against the early front-runners however firm a favourite they might

appear; once the final short-list is known put your shirt on YouGov's Tory member polls.

7. **In Liberal Democrat leadership elections put your money on the candidate who is most well known.**
Be warned about following the betting. Punters might be following other punters who they think are in the know when in fact the market is totally wrong.

8. **Capitalise on the confusion that national opinion polls do not cover Northern Ireland.**
The vote share markets tend to be on an all-UK basis, while the opinion polls always exclude Northern Ireland where there is a very different political culture. This can make a 1-2% difference in what the main parties get and might offer betting value.

9. **Make money from the media cliché in the second campaign week of a general election campaign that there is massive voter apathy**
It has almost become a media cliché that in the second week of a general election campaign the pundits start saying there is massive voter apathy. Suggestions of very low turnout will be widespread. If there are markets on what the percentage will be it is wise to go on the higher side because it is only in the final few days that the public starts taking notice.

10. **Finally, ...if there's a betting market on something happening to David Blunkett always take the bet.**

At the start of December 2004 you could have got 7/2 on him being out of a job over the Kimberley Quinn affair. That was a winner. Then 5/1 was being offered on Blunkett returning to the Cabinet during 2005. He was appointed Works and Pensions Secretary in the immediate aftermath of the 2005 general election and the bet proved to be a winner. Then in December 2005 there was another Blunkett "not surviving" market when you could have got 7/4 on him not making it through the month. Again a winner.

Appendices

Appendices

Major World Elections 2007-2010

French Presidential Election April-May 2007

February 2007 prices

Candidate	Price (Feb 2007)
Nicolas Sarkozy	0.9/1
Ségolène Royal	1.3/1
Francois Bayrou	25/1
Jean-Marie Le Pen	54/1

Betting tactics and the election system

The method by which France elects its President could have been specially designed to make it interesting for betting! There are two rounds of voting – the first when a dozen or more hopefuls put their names forward, and the second which is a run-off between the two heading the leader board after round one.

It is often said that the French,

> "vote with their hearts at the first ballot but with their heads in the second"

In 2002, of the 17 candidates on the ballot all but 7 registered less than 5% of the votes each. This led to a massive splintering of the left wing vote, and the final election that everybody had been expecting – Jacques Chirac versus Lionel Jospin – did not happen. Jospin came third, less than 200,000 votes behind the Front National's Jean-Marie Le Pen. Jacques Chirac then went on to win the runoff by 82% -18%.

That has had a very big effect on French left-wing politics and will, I believe, help Ségolène Royal in 2007. For the left is not going to run the risk of a socialist candidate not being in the final run off and Royal will chalk up a substantially bigger first round share than Jospin's 16% in 2002.

If the squeeze is great enough then Royal could even end up ahead of Sarkozy on the first ballot which could give her campaign a boost for the second round. Those wanting to back her will probably get the best prices before the first vote; those going for Nicolas Sarkozy would be advised to wait until afterwards.

What I think will happen

Although, as I write in February 2007, Nicolas Sarkozy is pulling ahead in the polls, I am not fully convinced that he will make it. For, as well as the memory of 2002 on her side, Ségolène Royal also has her gender.

History shows that, generally, whenever the proposition is put to electorates that their country should have a woman leader for the first time, they have voted for the female candidate. When it comes to the crunch at the final stage of an electoral process, voters seem to like the idea of having an elected woman leader. This has been true in the UK, Ireland, New Zealand, Germany, Iceland, Pakistan, Israel, India, Sri Lanka and many other countries. If the form-book is to be believed then France will join them.

The women who have failed in general elections, are those like Kim Campbell in Canada in 1992 who was Prime Minister already when she fought her first general election.

US Presidential Election November 2008

February 2007 prices

Democratic nomination

Candidate	Price (Feb 2007)
Hillary Clinton	1.14/1
Barack Obama	3.7/1
John Edwards	5.4/1
Bill Richardson	22/1
Tom Vilsack	74/1

Republican nomination

Candidate	Price (Feb 2007)
John McCain	1.9/1
Rudolf Giuliani	9/2
Mitt Romney	5/1
Mike Huckerbee	24/1
Sam Brownback	28/1
Chuck Hagel	33/1
Condoleeza Rice	33/1
George Pataka	64/1

Winning Party 2008 Presidential Race

Party	Price (Feb 2007)
Democrats	0.8/1
Republicans	1.2/1

President 2008

Candidate	Price (Feb 2007)
Hillary Clinton	2/1
John McCain	10/3
Barack Obama	11/2
John Edwards	7/1
Rudolf Giuliani	10/1
Al Gore	12/1
Mitt Romney	12/1
Condoleezza Rice	20/1
Joseph Biden	25/1
Bill Richardson	28/1
Evan Bayh	33/1
Mike Huckabee	33/1
Sam Brownback	33/1
Russ Feingold	50/1
Chuck Hagel	50/1

Betting tactics and the election system

A key element in betting on US politics is to be careful of "following the money". The fact that a particular candidate is doing well in the betting in the UK probably means less now than it did four years ago, after the massive clamp-down on Americans taking part in online gambling.

Before, there were ways that US citizens could avoid the limitations and, certainly, some of their betting activity took place in UK markets, which inevitably had an impact on prices. But no more. Following the actions against certain UK betting executives while travelling in the US, non-US betting companies are taking extraordinary measures to stop American citizens using their services.

A good starting point for a campaign four years hence, is the party conventions in the August or September to endorse the name of the individual who will be fighting the November election. For it is during the speeches and the razzmatazz that future party stars are born. The black senator from Illinois Barack Obama came to public notice at the Democratic convention in July 2004 when he made a barn-stormer of a speech in support of John Kerry. His contribution impressed many, and it was not long after George Bush's second victory that he was being tipped for 2008. At the time you could have got a bet on at for 50/1.

At these sorts of prices so far out it makes sense to choose two or three possible contenders for speculative bets. The best sources of information are the web sites of US newspapers as well as the news magazines, such as *Time* and *Newsweek*. These two love to have featured the eventual winner on their cover a few years earlier.

Opinion polls prior to the election year itself are often tests of name recognition and can mislead. Throughout 2003 the former Governor of Vermont, Howard Dean, had swept to prominence and raised a lot of money after a brilliant campaign using the internet. By January 1st 2004 he was a tight odds-on favourite to get the nomination, even before a single person had cast a vote in his favour.

When they did, it all went flat. His first hurdle was the Iowa caucus on January 19, when party supporters gather at hundreds of separate places across the state to discuss amongst themselves the strengths and weaknesses of the contenders. This comes at the start of the cycle and has proved to be very influential. Dean found himself picking up just 18% from this process, against John Kerry who got 38% and John Edwards on 32%.

Watch Iowa very closely for both the Republican and Democratic races; it is here that the weaknesses of the different contenders are probed very closely. Will Democrats be ready to risk it with a woman or a black man? Will the Republicans find that John McCain's age stands against him?

The way Iowa decides is very different from most other states, where the choice is made by ballot in what are known as 'primaries'.

A new feature for the 2008 will be the primaries that are likely to take place on the first Tuesday in the February. A large number of states have agreed to move their primaries to that date and it might be that they cover more than half the entire population of the US. After what is being billed "Super Super-Tuesday" we will have a pretty good idea who the two parties are choosing. Political gamblers in the nomination markets, unfortunately, will have to wait until the party conventions before they can get hold of their winnings.

The choice of the next President itself is decided by the electoral college that is made up of representatives from each of the states based on what happens on polling day. Everything focuses on a handful of potential swing states and how the voting has gone there.

A huge amount of betting can take place after the voting is over and while the count is taking place.

Be warned: the exit polls (surveys of opinion that take place after people have voted at the polling stations themselves) can be misleading. Generally the early numbers overstate the Democrats, although it is possible that compensatory measures will be introduced by the pollsters in 2008.

What I think will happen

The climate of opinion in America, as seen by the 2006 Mid-Term elections, is moving away from the Republicans; I expect the next President of the United States to be a Democrat. As I write, in February 2007, the front runners in the democrat race are Hillary Clinton, Barack Obama and John Edwards. Any one of these, I believe, would beat any of the Republican hopefuls of Mitt Romney, John McCain or Rudolf Giuliani.

My money is on Barack Obama who I first backed at 50/1 in May 2005 and who I think will come out of the Iowa test very well.

UK General Election – some time before June 2010

February 2007 prices

Size of majority

Seat majority	Con	Lab
1-25	13/2	7/1
26-50	10/1	11/1
51-75	12/1	14/1
76-100	14/1	20/1
101-125	20/1	25/1
126-150	25/1	33/1
More than 150	25/1	33/1
No overall majority	6/5	

Party with most seats

Party	Price (Feb 2007)
Conservative Party	0.86/1
Labour Party	5/4
Liberal Democrat Party	100/1

Note: The above market means 'the party with the most seats', not necessarily the party that forms the government.

My prediction
for the general election and suggested betting tactics

At the time of writing Tony Blair is still leader of the Labour Party and Prime Minister. The big unknown is how his successor will be regarded by the electorate. Will the new person be able to counter the prevailing mood of a desire for change and help boost the party's poll ratings?

What is apparent is that, although Labour slumped in the final months of Tony Blair's period in office, the voters appeared far from convinced about the Conservative alternative. My guess is that the next UK general election will end up with no party having an overall majority.

What is hard for the Conservatives is that the mathematics of the electoral system means that they need a minimum 5-6% lead on votes, just to be sure of being ahead of Labour on seats. This is the average poll lead that the party is enjoying as I write.

So a very tight general election looks likely. Political gamblers wanting to bet on the number of seats each party will end up with are going to have to study the records of pollsters and have an understanding of how the various seat calculators work.

Accuracy of the opinion polls

One factor that could produce a surprise is the long standing tendency of UK polling firms, when tested against real results, to over-state the Labour share.

Based on their performance over several general elections, I will be putting my money on ICM as the best measure of Conservative support. For the Labour share I will be looking at what the lowest projections are from all the pollsters and taking that as my starting point. If the gap using this approach is more than 6% then the Tories will probably end up with most seats. If it is less than 4.5% then my money would be on Labour. The hard call is going to be if the gap is between these two numbers which I think is quite likely.

Lib-Dems

There are also the Liberal Democrats to think about. Given the expected 'time for change' mood, I sense that they will do well holding onto most of their gains chalked up in 1997, 2001 and 2005, but they could make further inroads in some Labour seats. They could be helped by Conservative supporters being more likely than in previous years to vote tactically when the outcome would mean depriving Labour of the seat.

So unless there is a sea-change in opinion when Labour's new leader takes over, my forecast is that we could see a general election with an outcome along the following lines.

Party	seats
Conservative Party	286
Labour Party	272
Liberal Democrat Party	60
Others	32

If the outcome is in this area then I think that David Cameron would try to form a minority administration offering enough "olive branches" to the Liberal Democrats and others to get a limited programme through. This would not upset him too much, as the parliamentary arithmetic would act as a defence against the right-wingers in his party who would be pushing for a more radical programme.

Online Information Sources

Key blogs

Blogs are becoming an increasingly important part of political communication and are likely to have a big impact on political outcomes. Those betting on politics should follow them carefully, but with a touch of scepticism. For along with the rise of blogs has also come the rise of what has become known as *astroturfing*.

The Wikipedia definition of astroturfing is:

> *In politics and advertising, the term astroturfing describes formal public relations (PR) campaigns that seek to create the impression of being a spontaneous, grassroots behavior. Hence the reference to the "AstroTurf" (artificial grass) is a metaphor to indicate "fake grassroots" support.*

> *The goal of such a campaign is to disguise the agenda of a client as an independent public reaction to some political entity—a politician, political group, product, service, event. Astroturfers attempt to orchestrate the actions of apparently diverse and geographically distributed individuals, by both overt ("outreach," "awareness," etc.) and covert (disinformation) means. Astroturfing may be undertaken by anything from an individual pushing their own personal agenda through to highly organised professional groups with financial backing from large corporations.*

You have been warned!

- **Politicalbetting.com**
  This is my site, set up in March 2004, to provide an information service and forum for those interested in betting on, or forecasting, political outcomes. With thousands of daily visitors, many of whom contribute to the discussions, it has become a great resource. The main challenge is that if good value bets are mentioned then they are not likely to last long. Bookmakers as well as punters also visit the site.
  www.politicalbetting.com

- **Guido Fawkes**
  This is the site of Guido – the most popular UK political blogger – who often moves into areas where others are reluctant to tread. Whether you agree with him or not this is a must read. His stories can and do affect betting markets.
  www.5thnovember.blogspot.com

- **By-Elections**
  The by election blog is usually only active when UK by elections are in the offing but has built up a good reputation as a good news source. **www.by_elections.blogspot.com**

- **ConservativeHome**

  ConservativeHome describes itself as "the unofficial home of the Tory grassroots" and came to the fore during the Conservative leadership election in 2005. Very comprehensive and a good read for all interested in politics and forecasting outcomes.

  www.conservativehome.com

- **Iain Dale's Diary**

  Run by the former owner of Politico's Bookshop, and now journalists and broadcaster, Iain Dale's Diary has become the model of what a good political blog should be. It gets a very large audience and attracts many comments.

  www.iaindale.blogspot.com

- **Indigo Council**

  Run by a public affairs consultancy the Indigo Council Blog is daily updated and provides a comprehensive source of what is going on in local government throughout the UK.

  www. indigopublicaffairs.wordpress.com

- **LibDem**

  This is a site that takes the best of a range of blogs from Liberal Democrats and is usually a good summary. It is a great place to look during parliamentary by elections and you can often get a sense of whether a spectacular victory is in the offing by the level of activity.

  www.libdemblogs.co.uk

- **LabourHome**
  The Labour version of ConservativeHome that was started later but has become a very big and informative site.
  www.labourhome.org

- **Paul Linford**
  Run by the former lobby journalist, Paul Linford, this is probably the best blog on Labour party matters. Paul has original insights and is a leader rather than a follower of received opinion. If Paul suggests that something might happen then you ought to consider for your betting. **www.paullinford.blogspot.com**

Odds comparison sites

- **bestbetting**
  One of the first of the betting odds search engines with prices from tens of thousands of events being updated by the minute from the main on-line bookmakers. Lots of special features including historical data that can help in spotting trends.
  http://odds.bestbetting.com

- **Oddschecker**
  Similar to Bestbetting but its political section is sometimes not as comprehensive.
  www.oddschecker.com

Wikipedia

The free online encyclopaedia has a vast array of data which are useful sources for political punters. Two areas I refer to frequently are:-

- http://en.wikipedia.org/wiki/List_of_UK_by-elections
  Probably the best collation of UK by election results that there is online.

- http://en.wikipedia.org/wiki/UK_general_election_2005
  Almost every election that takes place in the world gets its own Wikipedia pages – this one is my first port of call when I want to refer back to the 2005 UK general election.

Seat predictors

- **UK Elect**
  UK Elect is a long-standing site, some of which is only available on subscription that produces regular predictions on UK general elections.
  www.ukelect.co.uk

- **Electoral Calculus**
  One of the leading Commons seat predictors. Former Cambridge University, and now city mathematician, Martin Baxter, maintains this site with an impressive range of options and information. Martin's seat calculator takes a different approach from the others.
  www.electoralcalculus.co.uk

- **UK Polling Report**

  UK Polling Report is a blog on polls run by Anthony Wells, as well as an archive of polling data covering more than just the UK. It also has its own downloadable seat predictor.

  http://ukpollingreport.co.uk

- **ScotlandVotes**

  This is good resource for predicting what party vote shares will lead to at the elections for the Scottish Parliament.

  www.scotlandvotes.com

Polling data

- **ICM**

  A good summary table showing all ICM polls for the Guardian since 1984.

  www.icmresearch.co.uk/reviews/vote-intention-reports/guardian-report.asp

- **Ipsos-Mori**

  The Ipsos-Mori chart reports on its polls going back to 1979.

  www.mori.com/polls/trends/voting-all-trends.shtml

- **UK Polling Report**

  UK Polling Report's main UK voting intention chart is probably the best starting point to find out the latest polls or to seek findings on specific issues.

  www.ukpollingreport.co.uk/blog/voting-intention/

Election results

- **United Kingdom Election Results**

  United Kingdom Election Results of one form or another over the past 120 years are included in this excellent resource. If you want to know what share of the popular vote the Liberal chalked up in the 1885 General Election this is the place to come.

  www.election.demon.co.uk

- **Local Authority by election results**

  Many people look to the local council by elections that take place up and down the country each week as a good pointer for national trends. This site is updated weekly and had good historical records.

  www.gwydir.demon.co.uk/byelections/

- **British Parliamentary Constituency database**

  An extraordinary resource that is downloadable is the British Parliamentary Constituency database, 1992-2005. It is a massive file but almost everything that you might want to know about a particular seat is available here.

  http://ksghome.harvard.edu/~pnorris/Data/Data.htm

Leading Betting Websites

Traditional bookmakers

The following traditional bookmakers usually maintain a range of political markets.

Bet 365
www.bet365.com

BlueSquare
www.bluesq.com

Corals
www.coral.co.uk

Ladbrokes
www.ladbrokes.com

Paddy Power
www.paddypower.com

SkyBet
www.skybet.com

Sporting Odds
www.sportingodds.com

Stan James

www.stanjames.com

Totesport

www.totesport.com

Betting exchanges

These betting exchanges usually have political markets.

Betfair

www.betfair.com

Betdaq

www.betdaq.com

Back and Lay

www.backandlay.com

Intrade

www.intrade.com

Spread-betting operators

These are the spread-betting firms that almost always run political markets.

Bethilo
www.bethilo.com

Binary Bet
www.binarybet.com

Cantor Spreadfair
https://cantor.spreadfair.com

IG Index
www.igindex.co.uk

Sporting Index
www.sportingindex.com

Glossary of Betting Terms

Arbitrage (to "arb")
Making a combination of bets so that if one bet loses another wins.

Back
To bet that an option or outcome will happen is to *back* it.

Banker
When a selection is fancied very, very strongly it is said to be a *banker bet*.

Bet slip
A paper form or web site page that shows placed bets.

Bookmaker
Someone who accepts bets and pays you if you win.

Buy
A spread betting term meaning that your are betting that the higher value of a quote will be exceeded. Thus if the Liberal Democrats are quoted at 54-57 seats for the general election and the final total is 62 seats – you win the actual number minus the buy level multiplied by your stake.

Decimal odds
The format that is mostly used by betting exchanges and is your return on a winning bet including your stake. Thus a successful £10 bet at 5 will produce a return of £50; the equivalent to fractional odds of 4/1.

Evens

The fractional odds of 1/1. A bet of £5 at evens would win £5, and your returns would be £10 (which includes your stake back.)

Event

The event or outcome that bets are placed on.

Favourite

The option in a betting market deemed by the Bookies to be most likely to win. It will have the shortest odds.

IBAS

The *Independent Arbitration Betting Service*. An arbitration service, which was launched to deal with betting disputes between punters and bookmakers.

Joint favourite

In a situation where outcomes are regarded with equal favour by the bookies (i.e. they have a supposedly equal chance of winning), they are said to be joint favourites.

Lay

What the bookmaker or betting exchange gambler does when he/she accepts bets from a punter.

Market

The betting available (odds offered) on any event.

Mid Point

Spread betting term. The point value exactly between the *buy* and *sell* prices.

Odds

The ratio of potential winnings to stake offered by a bookmaker. The odds represent the chance of your selection winning. So odds of 4/1 (spoken as "4 to 1") means that the bookmaker thinks there is a 1 in 5 chance of winning. For every £1 you bet at these odds, you will receive £4 profit. Odds can be expressed as a fraction, (as in our example of 4/1) or as a decimal. 4/1 is expressed as a decimal odds of 5.0, in which case you just multiply the decimal form of the odds by your stake to find out your total winnings (including your stake).

Odds On

Price where you have to stake more than the amount you expect to win. If a candidate, a party or other outcome is very likely to win, the odds may be shorter than Evens (1/1), for example, 1/2. Such odds are spoken as "2 to 1 on". In this example, odds of 1/2 mean you will win £1 for every £2 staked – and so you will get a total return of £3.

Outsider

The betting outcome considered by the bookmaker to have less chance of winning than others. Although outside chances do sometimes win, they are priced long *because* they don't really have much chance.

Over-round

The bookie's profit is determined by how much over 100% the total odds add up to. So if all the odds on all the options add up to 125%, that 25% theoretically represents the bookie's profit on every 100 pounds wagered. This is the *over-round*.

Punter

The term used to describe someone who places bets.

Punt

Another way of saying to bet.

Price

Another term for odds.

Sell

Spread betting term, meaning that you are betting that the lower value of a spread betting quote will not be reached.

Shorten

Odds that reduce, say from 5/1 to 3/1, are said to have *shortened*.

Value

The term referring to good odds that do not represent the real chances of an outcome happening, and are higher than would be expected. If you've worked out what you think are the real odds, and the bookie is giving longer odds, this is a value bet.

Glossary of Political Terms

Backbencher
An MP or Peer who holds no official position in the government or senior position in an opposition party. The backbenchers sit on the back benches on either side of the Chamber.

Constituency
The UK is divided into areas called constituencies, each one with an MP in the House of Commons to represent them. At the 2005 General Election there were 646 constituencies; this is due to increase to 650 as a result of a review of the boundaries due to be finalised in 2007. A citizen of a constituency is known as a *constituent*.

Despatch Box
Inside each House, there is a Despatch Box on each side of the Table that separates the government from the Opposition. Ministers and Shadow Ministers speak to the House from these boxes.

General Election
The process whereby the whole House of Commons stands for election at the same time. Each of the constituencies in the UK chooses an MP to represent it, and the party who wins the majority of constituencies (seats) forms the government. The leader of that party becomes Prime Minister and its ministers make up the new Cabinet. General elections are held at least every five years; the exact timing is decided by the Prime Minister, there is often an election before the full five years has elapsed.

Hung Parliament

A term used to describe a situation where no single party has enough MPs to form a majority in the House of Commons.

Majority

A term used in an election, where it refers to the margin that the candidate with the highest number of votes has over the candidate coming second. To win a seat a candidate need only have a majority of 1.

Minister

Departmental Ministers, Ministers of State and Junior Ministers. Ministers make up the government and are usually members of the House of Commons or the House of Lords. Departmental Ministers are in charge of government departments. Departmental Ministers in the Cabinet are generally called Secretary of State but some have special titles such as Chancellor of the Exchequer. Ministers of State and Junior Ministers assist the Departmental Ministers in charge of the department.

MP

A Member of Parliament (MP) is elected by a particular constituency in the UK to represent them in the House of Commons. An MP will represent all the people in their constituency and can ask government ministers questions, speak about issues in the House of Commons and propose and vote on new laws.

Opposition

These are the political parties in Parliament other than the government party, and are so called as they sit on the benches opposite the government in the chambers. The party who received the second highest number of seats in the House of Commons (therefore the largest opposition party) is known as Her Majesty's Loyal Opposition, or the Official Opposition. The leader of this party is called the Leader of the Opposition, and is entitled to sit on the front bench, close to the despatch box. In the House of Lords, the Leader of the Opposition heads the main party opposing the Government.

Prime Minister's Questions (PMQs)

The Prime Minister answers 30 minutes of questions from MPs in the House of Commons every Wednesday from 12.00pm. The Leader of the Opposition is allowed to ask a total of six questions and the leader of the Liberal Democrats two.

Queen's Speech

At the start of every session of Parliament, the Monarch reads an Address written by the government outlining their policies and bills for the following session. This is known as the Queen's (or King's) Speech, and is read during the State Opening of Parliament in the House of Lords.

Shadow Cabinet

This is the name given to the group of senior members of the official Opposition party in the House of Commons who would form the cabinet if they were to come to power after a general election. Each of these MPs is appointed to shadow one of the members of the Cabinet, so that every Department can be scrutinised fully.

Further glossary details for both politics and betting can be found at: www.intersites.co.uk/10649/

Index

Arbitrage ('Arb') 113,115,116,189
Back and Lay 42,43,44,187
Bestbetting 146,182
Bet 365 186
Betdaq 187
Betfair 14,16,22,42,44,46,54,55,70,114,115,153,154,157,187
Bethilo 188
Betting duty 57
Betting exchanges 20,28,32,37,39,40,41,44,45,54,55,57,70,153,
187,189
Betting odds search engines 27,146,182
Betting On The Opinion Polls 95
Betting Vehicle 7,25
Betting Websites 186
Binary Bet 188
Blair, Tony 49,50,53,67,69,87,88,89,109,114,115,176
Blogs 179
BlueSquare 186
Bookmakers 7,13,16,25-27,29,31,32,37,38,39,44-46,55,57,73,114,
152,157,186,190
BrandIndex 96
British Polling Index 122,123
Brown, Gordon 90,113,114,141
Cameron, David 2,80,83,84,85,86,127,141,142,178
Campbell, Sir Menzies 106,129,131
Cantor Spreadfair 49,55,188
Capital gains tax 56
Chris Huhne 91,92,108,129,132,151
Combination bets 113
Communicate Research 122,123,139
Conservatives 82
Corals 186
Credit account spread betting 31,32
Credit accounts 52
Currency 46
Daily Telegraph 16,123,125
Davis, David 2,80,83,85,110,127,128

Deposit account spread betting 30,32
Deposit accounts 51
General elections – the different markets 68
George W. Bush 13,15,17,134
Glossary of Betting Terms 189
Glossary of Political Terms 193
Good value 149,150,151,158
Guardian, The 95,123,125,132,184
High street bookmakers 25,26,32
ICM 122,123,125,136,138,139,177,184
IG Index 47,50,96,188
Income tax 56
Independent,The 123,132
Intrade 45,46,96,187
Ipsos Mori 122,123
Kerry, John 13,105,134,172,173
Labour 86
Ladbrokes 186
Legalisation 9
Liberal Democrats 90
Macmillan, Harold 10
NOP 122,123
Obama, Barack 2,170,172,174
Oddschecker 146,182
Opening odds 37
Opinion polls 19,72,95,122,124,130,136,161,173,177
Paddy Power 186
Party Leadership Contests 79
Past vote weighting 123,124,137
Personal bias 15
Personal ratings 142
Political markets 9,27,28,35,40,45,47,49,186,188
Political pollsters 122
Populus 122,123,125,127,137,138,139
Risk 1,7,32,37,42,46,54,56,62,67,71,133,157,158
SkyBet 186
Smith, Iain Duncan 83,85,109,110,126

Sporting Index 188
Sporting Odds 186
Spread Betting 47
Stan James 187
Terms 38,44,152,156
Times, The 123,125
Totesport 187
Trading bets 20,22
Traditional Betting 33
Traditional bookmakers 27,32,37,38,44,49,70,186
Turnouts 138
UK General Election 16,61,63,123,136,175,176,183
UK Polling Report 66,75,126,184
US Presidential Election 17,134,170
Westminster By-Elections 94
William Hill 69,114,115,116
YouGov 85,89,93,96,122,123,125,126,129,130,139